Contents

Editor Greg Payne

Design Editor Liz Wright

Origination Sally Robinson

Published by Greenlight Publishing
The Publishing House, 119 Newland Street
Witham, Essex CM8 1WF
Tel: 01376 521900 **Fax:** 01376 521901
mail@greenlightpublishing.co.uk www.greenlightpublishing.co.uk

Printed in Great Britain
ISBN 1 897738 24 2
© 2005 Rainer Pudill & Clive Eyre

Front cover: Gallo-Belgic Ambiani type E gold stater.

Foreword

Dr. Rainer Pudill M.A. was my pupil when I was Professor of Ancient History at Düsseldorf University. But he was no ordinary undergraduate. After many years as a research scientist he came to the university as a mature student. I soon discovered that he had a longstanding interest in, and a detailed knowledge of, the ancient world; and that his expertise in ancient numismatics far exceeded my own.

He gave some excellent seminar papers, and meanwhile had been publishing articles in numismatic periodicals. Some time after I retired, he sent me the typescript of an abundantly illustrated work on the Celtic coinage of Britain. I am delighted that his friend, Clive Eyre, has now provided a very readable English translation. This work places Ancient British coinage in its context, with a lucid introduction on the origins and culture of the Celts, as revealed by Greek and Latin authors and by archaeology.

In recent years, some prefer to write "so-called Celts". Of course, ancient writers were not always precise. The Greeks, for example, in due course found it difficult to distinguish between the Keltoi, Keltae, Galli or Galatae on the one hand and the Germani on the other, and persistently labelled the latter "Celts from beyond the Rhine". As Dr. Pudill emphasises, the Celtic peoples never formed a nation or political unity. But this is hardly surprising, given that they settled over such a wide area, from Portugal to Turkey, besides covering most of France, large parts of central Europe and northern Italy - and the British Isles.

Much remains uncertain, of course; for example, the period when some of them first arrived in Britain. Still, Celtic is a legitimate term for the Britons of the Iron Age - the evidence of ancient British names, of both persons and places, supplied not least by the coins presented and discussed in this book, shows that the inhabitants of our island at that time spoke a language essentially the same as that of their continental neighbours (and that modern Welsh has developed from ancient British). Dr. Pudill does not enter into this debate: he supplies the evidence and is careful to point out where it is uncertain.

As well as discussing Celtic culture and the coins of the Britons, he also includes accounts of the Roman invasions, by Caesar and Claudius, and of British resistance or rebellion. Such narratives are based, inevitably, on writings of the conquerors. Tacitus and Cassius Dio invented some rousing and defiant speeches by British leaders, but this is no substitute for our lack of an authentic British voice. But the coins of the Britons, so vividly portrayed and analysed here, do remind us that before the Romans occupied much of the island its civilisation was already at a high level.

How Britain would have developed if Rome had left it alone is an intriguing question. The likely answer, at the political level, is that the sons of Cunobelinus, whom Suetonius called "king of the Britons", would have created an even wider dominion than their father had. The Atrebates, Dobunni and Iceni, and other peoples further north, notably the Brigantes, assumed at first that the superpower would protect them from subjection to the largest British state, and leave them "independent". They were soon disillusioned.

This book helps us to get a better impression of the British peoples before they were absorbed into the great empire as a province. Only the northernmost Britons, of Caledonia, were to escape this fate, or, some may prefer, were to be denied this privilege, of "becoming Romans" instead of "barbarians".

Prof. Anthony Birley, FSA, Vindolanda

Introduction

The roots of the Celtic race are shrouded in mystery. All we can say with certainty is that they were undoubtedly of Indo-European origin. Whether the people of the Urnfield cultures of Central Europe (1200-800 BC) can really be considered as Celts is still under dispute - the term "proto-Celts", occasionally applied to them, makes clear the uncertainty of their classification. However, there is excellent archaeological evidence for the Celts both of the Hallstatt period (circa 800-450 BC), which takes its name from the cemetery discovered in the Salzkammergut in Austria, and also for the following period, called La Tène after the principal find spot by Lake Neuenburger in western Switzerland.

The transition from the Urnfield culture to the Hallstatt coincides with the beginning of the Iron Age in Central Europe. In the 7th century before Christ, bronze gave way to iron; this was a harder metal, more suitable for weapons, tools, armour and household goods of all kinds, and marked a milestone in technology. As well as being much harder, iron was easy to work, and these properties gave the Celts immense advantages, both social and economic. The tribal rulers and chieftains who controlled the copper trade, essential in the production of bronze (and also tin), which came from mines in Britain, now found their importance slipping away. Now every town or *oppidum* could begin its own production of iron goods, both utilitarian and luxury.

However, this process was a slow one, extending over a long period, and it did not in any way stop imports from southern Europe; neither did it affect cultural exchanges with the Mediterranean civilisations. Luxury goods, such as bronze-ware, pottery, coral, jewellery and wine - imported mainly through the Greek colony at Massalia (modern day Marseille) - now began to reach every level of society in the Celtic lands. These imports were paid for mainly with raw materials such as iron and gold, and also with finished goods, such as weapons and textiles, as well as with hides, honey and salt - a highly prized commodity in those days.

After the late 6th century BC, the Celts began to migrate from their homelands in various directions. By the 5th century they had settled in what is now southern Germany, Austria, Switzerland, France and the Czech Republic, as well as parts of the Iberian peninsula and Britain.

In about 400 BC some tribes found their way across the Alpine passes into northern Italy, where they became a stubborn and a dangerous threat to Rome - the siege of the city from 387 to 386 by the Celtic warlord Brennus was a traumatic event for the Romans, and had far reaching consequences.

Other Celtic tribes moved down the Danube to Thrace, and thence into the Crimean peninsula. After the famous sacking of Delphi in 279 BC, some 20,000 of them passed through Greece and crossed the Bosporus into Asia Minor, where first they served as mercenaries for various rulers, and then finally settled in central Anatolia.

They are best known to us today through the **Epistle to the Galatians** of St. Paul. Centuries later, St. Jerome, writing in about AD 400, notes that the people he called "Galatoi" still spoke a Celtic language.

For a period of at least 500 years the history of Western Europe was dominated by the Celts. Their territory reached its greatest extent in about 250 BC, but they never managed to achieve either political or administrative unity, and neither could they ever have been called a single nation state. Mainly, this was because they were never one people in the true sense of the word, but rather just a cultural grouping, united by a common language, a way of life, tradition, beliefs and mythology.

A characteristic style, tending towards abstractness and stylisation, distinguishes Celtic art and coinage from contemporary Roman and Greek productions. The Celts never really took to the art of writing, (although they did use a script adapted from the Greek alphabet for some short inscriptions), and produced no literature of any significance before the post-Roman era. This makes archaeological finds all the more important and their coins, in particular, are unique as sources of information.

Our knowledge of this race - variously called Keltoi, Keltai, Galatai, Celtae, and Galli - derives mainly from Greek and Roman sources. The earliest mention of the Celts is found in the works of the geographer Hecataeus of Miletus, and the historian Herodotus, writing in about 500 and 450 BC respectively. Later reports are found in the historians Polybius and Poseidonius, the geographer Strabo, and the travel writer Pausanias. But most important of all are the writings of Julius Caesar, the first ancient author who was able to distinguish between the Celts and the Germans. A keen observer, diplomat and politician, Caesar, with his *Bellum Gallicum*, (**The Gallic War**), has left us not only a report of his conquest of Gaul and the Celtic method of making war, but most importantly invaluable details about the Celtic peoples such as their customs, their habits, their religion, their way of life, and what he regarded as their strengths and weaknesses.

In spite of a somewhat one-sided view on Caesar's part, a lack of impartiality and a tendency to twist the truth at times, the reports of other ancient historians, scientists and writers agree with him on certain qualities of the Celtic peoples: their gallantry and courage, their generosity and hospitality, their loyalty and love of family life. But on the other hand, we also read of their lack of self-control, their unpredictability, their vanity and conceit, their unlimited desire for gain, and their cruelty.

Further information about the Celts is given us by Augustus, who in his *Res Gestae* (**My Achievements**) refers to some British kings by name, and by Livy, Suetonius, and Ammianus Marcellinus, who wrote in about AD 400. Although regarded nowadays as less reliable, the **History of the Romans** by the Greek-speaking historian Cassius Dio and the *Historia Augusta* are further sources.

But of particular importance to the history of Britain is the work of Tacitus about his father in law Agricola (*De Vita Iulii Agricolae*), which he completed in AD 98, and also his **Histories and Annals**. In his **Agricola**, Tacitus not only describes in detail the British campaigns of that great general and diplomat, but also gives us valuable information about the history, geography and ethnic make-up of the country.

Please Note
Coin illustrations are all twice actual size. (Actual dimensions are given in captions).

Gold stater of Philip II (359-336 BC) of Macedon.
This was the prototype of many Celtic coins.

Chapter 1

The Celtic Pantheon

Our knowledge of Celtic religious beliefs is very scanty. To a great extent this is because they did not see their gods as solid beings, but rather as abstract symbols, understandable only through their effects on human life. This view of the world of belief and the spirit is best seen in the Druidic cult, where the Druids were not only priests as we would understand the word - they also exercised moral and religious authority and were, in effect, a totally separate and elite social class.

The almost complete absence of any kind of written record is another reason why Celtic religion seems so strange to us today. Caesar tells us *"Their religion forbids the Druids to set down their teaching in writing, although for other purposes, public and private, the Greek alphabet may be used. They do not wish their teaching to become common knowledge, and they expect their* disciples to use memory alone." (**Gallic War** 6, 14).

From inscriptions in Gaul alone, the names of 374 Celtic gods are known to us. Most, however, had only local importance. Probably many were not separate deities, but rather different names and aspects of just a few gods, which all the Celtic tribes worshipped in common. Their principal gods are named by Caesar in his **Gallic War**, although with Roman names. This follows what Tacitus called the *interpretatio Romana,* by which foreign deities were identified with Roman ones, according to their natures and areas of interest. These were Mercury, Apollo, Mars, Jupiter and Minerva (**Gallic War** 6, 17). Unfortunately, Caesar omits to name the Celtic gods that he equated with the Roman ones, so that a proper identification, although eminently desirable, is not really possible.

However, Lucan, in his **Pharsalia**, gives the

Fig.1. Remi/Gaul, cast potin, 20mm, c.100-60 BC. DLT 8145.
Male figure seated facing cross-legged, torque in left hand.
Boar standing right, fibula and star above.
Leu AG, Zürich 86, May 2003, 84.

Fig.2. Senones/Gaul. Bronze unit, 17mm. c.60-50 BC.
DLT 7493.
YLLYCCI. Raven to left, behind pentagram and star.
Leu AG, Zürich 86, May 2003, 90.

names of the three principal Celtic gods. These are: Teutates (Celtic "God of the nation"), Taranis (Celtic "Thunder"), and Esus (Celtic "Lord").

It was probably Teutates whom Caesar associated with Mercury, and placed in the leading role. Teutates/Mercury was not only the god of travellers and of trade, but also, like the Germanic Wotan or Odin, a deity of the Underworld, who accompanied the souls of those who had died honourable deaths down to the Kingdom of the Dead. It was probably also this god whom Caesar referred to elsewhere as "Dispater", and "from whom, according to the Druids, all the Gauls are supposed to be descended". (**Gallic War** 6, 18). The alternative names Albiorix, "King of the Universe", and Toutiorix, "Lord of the Nation", underline his importance among the Celtic gods. The horse was the animal sacred to Teutates, but it was later joined by the ram. Soon the ram's horns, or the ram-headed serpent, came to symbolise this god. Possibly another aspect of Teutates was Lug, to whom Lugdunum, present day Lyon, owes its name. In the sagas of Ireland he appears as a noble warrior, in golden armour and helmet, accompanied by ravens, who served him as messengers.

Taranis was the God of Thunder and the Great Lord of Heaven, similar to the Roman Jupiter and the Germanic Thor, and was, like Teutates, represented by the horse. His own attribute was, however, the wheel, symbolising the sun, which we find on innumerable artefacts and coins. Its four spokes stand for the four seasons, and for the four points of the compass.

As the god of battles, in time of war or danger ritual human sacrifices were made to Taranis, and probably to other Celtic deities too. The so-called Ceremony of the Skulls particularly horrified the Romans, and was used by them for propaganda purposes. This was a ritual stretching back into pre-historic times, and involved the beheading of enemies, in the belief that one could thereby obtain for oneself their strength and skill. The head had for the Celts a great religious significance, because it was the seat of that which we today call the immortal soul. Often such severed heads were placed in shrines, or exhibited for display.

Fig.3. Catuvellauni and Trinovantes Cunobelin, gold quarter stater, 18mm, c.AD 10-43.
VA 1910.
Wreath and inscribed tablet. CAMVL.
Two Celticised horses left; four-spoked wheel. CVNOBELIN.
CNG 57, April 2001,1701.

Fig.4. Ambiani/Gaul, bronze unit 15mm, "Head of Apollo".
DLT 8403.
Celticised head left.
Severed head of enemy.
Cabinet des Médailles, Paris.

Fig.5. Roman Republic, Serg. Silus (109-108 BC.), denarius, 19mm.
Seaby 1, Sergia 1.
Head of Roma right.
Horseman galloping left, holding sword and head of barbarian.
Tkalek AG, Zürich 2001, 188.

Warrior with severed head
of enemy.

The fertility god Esus, who is perhaps another aspect of Teutates, is often depicted as a farmer. His plant was the mistletoe, and his animals the boar and the bull.

The stag god Cernunnos, "the horned one", also has much in common with Teutates and Esus. The antlers of the stag represented fertility and plenty, and the creature associated with him, the serpent, marks him as also being a god of the Underworld.

In second place in the list of Celtic deities mentioned by Caesar is Apollo, who in his function as the god of light and well-being probably equates to the Celtic Belenus, whose name means "bright", or "shining". As the guardian of springs and health-giving spas, he was worshipped in Aachen as Apollo Grannus.

The importance of iron smelting has already been stressed, and so it is not surprising that the Celts also worshipped a god of blacksmiths, even to the extent of placing him on their coins.

Like Hephaistos with the Greeks, and Vulcan among the Romans, so the Celtic god Gobniu guarded - deep beneath the mountains - the secrets of metal working and the hardening of iron.

Coins of Cunobelin and Dubnovellaunus bearing the so-called "metal worker" type (VA 2097-1. Sear 5347) were definitely not intended to represent simply a smith at work, or even to represent iron working in general. Really they were intended to honour Gobiu or Dispater, the father god of the Celts, in his function as master of the secret forces that lay beneath the earth. He was also the protector of miners, and the ruler of fire, the furnace and the art of metal working. According to the *interpretatio Romana*, this god of the Underworld was identified with Jupiter and Silvanus (Moreau 106). Closely related to Gobniu, or possibly even the same being, was Sucellus, the Celtic "Good Hammerer", and also the Irish hammer-god Dagda.

Of the greatest importance in Celtic religion was the worship of female deities. Like the great mother goddesses of other early civilisations, the "Queen of Heaven" Rigantona or Rigani had equal standing with the Father of the Gods. She probably corresponds to

Fig.6. Atrebates, Epillus (10 BC-AD 10) silver unit 12mm.
VA 416.
Celticised head right.
Boar right. EPPI COM F.
Leu AG Zürich 86, May 2003, 16.

Fig.7. Atrebates, Tincomarus (c.30-10 BC) silver unit 11mm.
VA 381.
Celtic head right.
Bull right; pellet-in-ring motif. TIN.
Chris Rudd, list 58, 2001, no.24.

Fig.8. Nervii/Gaul. Cast potin, 19mm, c.60-30 BC.
DLT 7527.
"Branch" flanked by pairs of dolphin-like ornaments. Tree of life?
Stag standing left within circle of annulets.
Leu AG, Zürich 86, May 2003, 80.

the mother goddess Rosmerta, worshipped in Gaul, and also to her British equivalent Birgit or Brigit, whose name means honour, worth or power.

Epona, known as the goddess of horses, was originally much more than that. Like the Greek Demeter, she could appear to men in the form of a mare. In earlier times she had been a goddess of the earth and its fruitfulness, but by Roman times she had been reduced to simply a horse goddess.

Like the divine triads of the Romans, mother or fertility goddesses appear in threes, the *matres* or *matronae*. As in other religions, the number three symbolised to the Celts not only the sun, the source of all life, but also perfection and power.

The British queen Boudica, widow of the Icenian king Prasutagus, is said by Cassius Dio to have launched the revolt of AD 60 in the name of the war-goddess Adraste, Andata or Andraste. This was a blood-soaked episode, costly to both sides in human life. At the start of the rebellion, in order to gain the

favour of the "invincible" goddess, the warlike royal widow sacrificed to her several captured Roman women, and then ordered the release of a caged hare, so as to learn from the course it took whether or not the goddess had accepted her offerings. (Dio 62, 6, 1). The companion of Andraste was the raven, a bird that loved battlefields and feasted upon the dead, and was therefore always associated with war and death. The raven became the symbol of Andraste, and appears on helmet decorations, the best-known example being the famous helmet of Ciumecti, in Romania. The bird is also frequently portrayed on Celtic coins. As well as Andraste, Camulos - a male god of war - was widely worshipped in Britain and Gaul.[1]

Triple faced Celtic deity. Vase from Bouvay, France.
Cabinet des Médailles, Bibliothèque Nationale, Paris.

Fig.9. Trinovantes, Dubnovellaunus (c.30-25 BC),
silver unit 14mm.
VA 178.
Horned animal left.
This coin betrays Roman influence in its portrayal of a
seated "metalworker".
Ashmolean Museum, Oxford.

Fig.10. Remi/Gaul. Bronze unit 15mm.
DLT 8040.
Three beardless jugate heads left.
Triga (?) galloping left.
Chris Rudd, list 66, 2002, no.9.

Remi/Gaul. Bronze unit 16mm.
DLT 8040.
Three beardless jugate heads left.

Unlike the Romans and Greeks, the Celts originally perceived their gods in the form of animals. Not until the late Iron Age did the Celtic gods take on human form, and then the animals tended to become their attributes or companions.

They also worshipped groves, trees, springs, streams, mountains, caves and standing stones, and even today in the names of some rivers we can detect the original Celtic name - for example, the Seine was the Celtic Sequana. Even some symbols or objects were sacred to the Celts - the double-headed axe, for example, which was believed to have magic powers. As late as the Christian Middle Ages, the axe was supposed to give a mystical protection against dis-

ease and the evil eye. Another such magic charm was the pentagram, or five-pointed star, which often appears upon Celtic coins and was for protection against evil spirits.[2.]

If we look at the Celtic gods through Roman eyes alone, we seriously risk a total failure to appreciate their original broad areas of activity, or even misunderstand them entirely. Moreau remarks in passing "that the strictly defined characters of the Roman gods mentioned by Caesar are a world away from the natures of the Celtic gods, whose spheres were vastly more extensive than those of the Roman gods, with whom he identified them". (Moreau 104).

Fig.11. Iceni. Bury type; Early silver unit 14mm, c.50-40 BC.
VA- dJ 82.
Goddess of war Andraste (?).
solar rosette above horse.
Chris Rudd, list 15, 1995, no.26.

Iceni, silver unit 15mm.
Goddess of war Andraste (?).
Chris Rudd, list 41, 1999, no.5.

Chapter 2

Mercenaries
& The First Celtic Coins

Their courage and steadiness caused the Celts to be greatly respected as fighting men. As early as the 6th century BC they are to be found as mercenaries in the service of the Etruscans and Carthaginians. In 369-68 BC they were fighting in Greece for the Syracusans; later in that century they took part in the wars of the Diadochi for the succession to Alexander's empire. In the "Great Expedition" of the year 280 BC entire armies of mercenaries passed through the Danube lands and Thrace to Anatolia, and even reached Egypt, where Ptolemy Philadelphos had 4,000 Gauls put to death on an island in the Nile, because he feared a revolt. Later, during Roman times, Celts fought on every battlefield of the Mediterranean world.

Mercenaries hired in the eastern Mediterranean lands in the late 4th and 3rd century BC were paid primarily in tetradrachms and gold staters of Philip II of Macedon.

From these returning mercenaries, and from trading links, which were mainly with Greek settlements and colonies, the Celts learned the advantages of a

Fig.12. Philip II of Macedon (359-336 BC), silver tetradrachm, 24mm.
Head of Zeus/Jupiter right.
Naked jockey (Olympionide) on horseback to right,
holding palm branch in his right hand.
R. Pudill.

Fig.13. Philip II of Macedon (359-336 BC), gold stater, 20mm.
Laureate head of Apollo.
Biga galloping to right.
Tkalek AG, Zürich 2000, 36.

cash economy. The gold and silver coinage which they began to strike themselves imitated mainly types they knew. Celtic coinage developed in different areas at varying speeds, depending on the type and volume of trade, and upon other geographical, economic and political factors. The first coins to be struck in Gaul, for example, were imitations of Massalian silver struck early in the 4th century BC.

While the Celts of eastern and southern Gaul preferred silver for their coins, the tribes of central and northern Gaul, and later the Arverni and Aedui, took as their model the gold coinage of Philip of Macedon, and initially they tried to copy it as closely as possible. But after the collapse of the Arverni alliance in 121 BC, various trends in style become apparent, differing from each other mainly in their levels of abstractness. The realistic portraits and reverse types of the originals become progressively more simplified, turning into purely geometric shapes, and finally becoming nothing more than ornamental patterns.

But to see them as degraded, degenerated or barbarous is to misunderstand them completely. An artistically independent and aesthetically appealing style was developing, and new subjects and patterns were coming into being. Through its reduction of the images to basic designs, it is almost as though Celtic coinage anticipates modern abstract art.

The Celtic tribes of Britain went even farther than the Gauls and the eastern Celts in their movement towards abstract and stylised design. In the 1st century BC they adopted the coinage of the Ambiani, imitated it, and later drastically simplified it.

The earlier gold coinage of this tribe, unusually large and weighing around 7.8gm, belongs without doubt to the most beautiful of Celtic numismatic art. Although much is clearly owed to the influence and character of the original, the Philippian stater, nonetheless the style is unmistakeably Celtic. The splendid treatment of the wreath and hair, which

Fig.14. Prototype: Massalia/Gaul, c.220-190 BC,
silver unit, 17mm.
Head of Artemis right.
Lion prowling right.
Leu AG, Zürich 77, 2000, 25.

Fig.15. Gallia Cisalpina, Type Massalia, silver drachm
16mm, mid 3rd century.
DLT 2126.
Head of Artemis to right.
Celticised lion (scorpion-like) right.
Chris Rudd, list 80, 2005, no.1.

Pablo Picasso, Head of a Woman, Boisgeloup 1933. Bronze, 16.5cm x 14cm. Private Collection.

Compare to the portrait on a silver coin of the Atrebatan king Commius, c.50-40 BC. (Chris Rudd, list 54, 2000, No.16.).

flows out in spiral curls and takes up more than half of the flan, is striking in the extreme. The charioteer on the reverse is now no more than implied, and the lettering has become part of the design. A sun symbol hints at the Ruler of Heaven, Taranis. On the later, lighter weight staters of the Ambiani, all that remains of the head is a blob, and the wreath and hair have become no more than a Y-shaped pattern. The horse on the reverse is made up of crescent shapes, and a square or a triangle represent its head.

Among the Continental tribes, the old system of trade, based upon barter, survived until the end of the 3rd century BC alongside the newer, money-based system, while in Britain it lasted until the second half of the 1st century BC. Not until the 2nd century before Christ did cash money become the principal method of payment and means of measuring value (considerably later in Britain).

In the period of transition from individual self-sufficiency to a money-based economy, the gold stater was used primarily for hoarding wealth, for paying tribute and settling war debts, or for buying luxury imports. Caesar informs us that these coins were also given as dowries (**Gallic War** 6, 19). Later, however, the introduction of smaller silver coins, and billon, potin, copper and bronze denominations, made it became possible to bring domestic trading and everyday transactions into a solely money based economy.

Dating and attributing most early Celtic coins, which have no legends, is difficult. As a general rule, they tend to be assigned, purely on the basis of numbers found, to the tribe in whose territory most are discovered (VA; Jones 50-55). We should not, however, speak of tribal coinages, because the concept of a state - with central rule and therefore a coining authority - just did not exist. Rather, local workshops just struck coins according to need and demand,

Fig.16. Ambiani/Gaul (Gallo-Belgic), (c.55 BC), gold stater 26mm.
DLT 7878; VA 10 var.
Celtic head of Apollo left, naturalistic face.
Celticised horse left, solar symbols.
Chris Rudd, list 20, 1996, no.2.

No	Fine	Very Fine	No	Fine	Very Fine	No	Fine	Very Fine
64	£220	£500	91	£130	£300	118	£40	£120
65	£275	£750	92	£125	£280	119	£160	£500
66	£325	£750	93	£140	£325	120	£40	£120
67	£250	£650	94	£50	£165	121	£140	£350
68	£220	£575	95	£300	£700	122	£45	£130
69	£550	£1400	96	£280	£650	123	£50	£150
70	£140	£325	97	£130	£275	124	£40	£120
71	£360	£900	98	£250	£700	125	£120	£250
72	£80	£200	99	£220	£500	126	£240	£600
73	£35	£90	100	£90	£350	127	£130	£275
74	£325	£800	101	£65	£200	128	£60	£180
75	£300	£800	102	£1500	£4000	129	£75	£200
76	£550	£1400	103	£50	£200	130	£280	£700
77	£140	£325	104	£40	£150	131	£200	£450
78	£70	£250	105	£90	£220	132	£75	£200
79	£475	£1350	106	£35	£125	133	£60	£180
80	£1500	£4000	107	£130	£325	134	£50	£160
81	£300	£850	108	£70	£230	135	£350	£850
82	£200	£650	109	£50	£200	136	£180	£550
83	£350	£900	110	£150	£400	137	£120	£300
84	£120	£260	111	£75	£260	138	£65	£150
85	£280	£700	112	£40	£150	139	£850	£2400
86	£160	£400	113	£20	£45	140	£175	£450
87	£60	£175	114	£150	£400	141	£280	£700
88	£60	£160	115	£100	£250	142	£3000	£7500
89	£220	£550	116	£850	£2400	143	£150	£375
90	£40	£130	117	£60	£180			

The Tribes & Coins of Celtic Britain
Price Guide

No	Fine	Very Fine	No	Fine	Very Fine	No	Fine	Very Fine
1	£ 60	£150	24	£1000	£2500	44	£650	£1600
2	£35	£90	25	£400	£900	45	£700	£1800
3	£650	£1800	26	£400	£900	46	£160	£500
4	£150	£400	27	£180	£500	47	£150	£350
5	£25	£60	28	£200	£460	48	£150	£400
6	£120	£300	29	£240	£550	49	£600	£1500
7	£90	£240	30	£250	£575	50	£450	£1100
8	£140	£350	31	£350	£800	51	£220	£575
9	£275	£650	32	£375	£1000	52	£225	£600
10	£45	£120	33	£160	£350	53	£220	£560
11	£75	£220	34	£60	£140	54	£150	£350
12	£160	£400	35	£25	£60	55	£120	£300
13	£375	£900	36	£120	£275	56	£110	£240
14	£60	£140	37	£60	£150	57	£75	£220
15	£80	£180	38	£350	£850	58	£65	£150
16	£600	£1700	39	£300	£800	59	£30	£75
17	£170	£375	40	£325	£800	60	£65	£150
18	£225	£500	41	£45	£120	61	£50	£130
21	£150each	£400 each	42	£55	£140	62	£30	£75
23	£180 each	£500 each	43	£35	£90	63	£140	£400

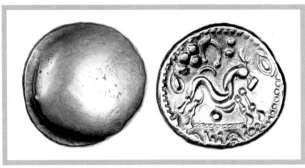

Fig.17. Ambiani Gallo-Belgic gold stater, 17mm, c.60-30 BC.
DLT 8710.
Plain.
Disjointed horse to right. Patterned exergue.
Chris Rudd, list 80, 2005, no.14.

which explains the widely varying precious metal content and also the abundance of imitations. Thus, we cannot speak of a single, unified Celtic coinage, and neither do we even know by what names the Celts called their coins. We make do by calling them by the names of their Greek and Roman equivalents (e.g. stater, drachma, denarius, quinarius), although sometimes we call them after their characteristic types, such as "cross coins" and "sheaf quinarii".

Celtic coinage came to an end, in Gaul at least, with the Roman conquest. The very last Celtic coinage in Britain is most likely a silver coin of Prasutagus, client king of the Iceni, and husband of the famous Boudica (de Jersey 52, no 88; VA 780-1).[3.]

Fig.18. Atrebates, c.55-45 BC, gold stater, 19mm.
VA 210, 212-5.
Celticised and abstract head of Apollo right.
Celticised horse right, with triple-tail, charioteer reduced to his arms; five-spoked wheel below horse.
Chris Rudd, list 27, 1997, no.27.

Fig.19. Increasing grades of abstraction on Celtic coins. The prototype is at left.

17

Chapter 3

Iron Bars & Ring Money

In Book Five of his **Gallic War**, Caesar mentions that the Britons, as well as using gold and copper coins, also traded with iron bars of determined weight (**Gallic War** 5, 12). These bars are found in every imaginable shape throughout the entire Celtic world. It is probable that they were in use in Britain from the 2nd century BC until the middle of the 1st. However, their weight, varying between 400gm and 500gm, and their inconvenient shapes - up to 900mm long in the case of the sword-shaped pieces - makes it unlikely that they were currency in the everyday sense. Rather it is likely that they were financial deposits or reserves, or were used as trade goods. The heavier examples, those weighing up to 5k, were four-sided ingots, pointed at each end. They are typified by those found at Augsburg and Nördlingen, as well at the Roman forts of Vindonissa, and Kaiseraugst in the Swiss canton of Aargau.[4.]

Another form of pre-coinage currency is the cast ring money, or rouelle, of gold, silver, bronze or lead. Hoard finds of intentionally broken examples, or cut pieces, indicate that ring money was used as religious offerings.

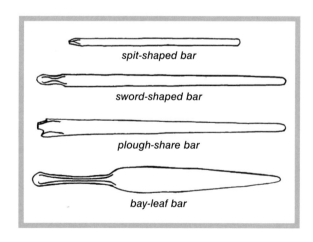

spit-shaped bar

sword-shaped bar

plough-share bar

bay-leaf bar

Fig.20 The four types of iron currency bars found in Britain. Designed primarily as a convenient way to store and carry smelted iron stock – each shape indicating a certain quality and certain place of origin – these bars appear to have had a secondary function as sacra moneta, as votive money for purchasing divine favours. Chris Rudd believes they were deposited as 'earth money' – money paid to Mother Earth in exchange for her bounty and protection. Chris Rudd, list 74, 2004, p.4-7.

Fig. 22 A symbolic life-cycle of iron (inner circle) in relation to earth (shaded), to iron implements and to their functions in the life-cycle of man (outer circle) in Iron Age Britain. Chris Rudd suggests that the burial of iron bars, 'reborn' as iron ore, may have symbolised man's own death and perhaps have served as a substitute for animal or human sacrifice. 'Earth money', Chris Rudd, list 74, 2004, p.4-7.

Fig. 21 Bay-Leaf Type iron currency bars, 45-59cm, Van Arsdell 5-7, dredged from Bourn Brook, near Grantchester, Cambs., c.1992-93.
'Their condition on discovery suggests that they had been quite neatly piled together and perhaps tied in a bundle…It is very tempting to picture the scene on the banks of the Bourn Brook, more than 2,000 years ago, when a group of eight currency bars resembling plough-shares were tied together and cast into the river. The details of this ceremony are unlikely ever to become clear, but perhaps it expressed thanks for a successful harvest, and ensured agricultural fertility would continue in the coming year.' Dr Philip de Jersey, 'Iron Age currency bars', Chris Rudd, list 50, 2000, p.2-4.

Fig. 24 The Spettisbury Ring, a Late Bronze Age penannular ring (traditionally called 'ring money'), 14mm, 7.09g, Van Arsdell 1-3, composed of 79 alternating stripes of gold and silver-rich gold, found near the Iron Age hillfort at Spettisbury, Dorset, 1999, not far from where iron currency bars had previously been found. Chris Rudd describes the ring as a 'remarkable feat of prehistoric technology' and suggests that it was worn as a nose-ring and also used as money. Current Archaeology 197, May/June 2005, p.215.
Photo Dorset County Museum.

Fig. 23 Spit-Shaped Type iron currency bars, 70-72cm, Van Arsdell 5-3, found near Cirencester, Glos. Cotswold collection, photo S.Beaumont.

Chapter 4

Caesar's Expeditions To Britain

After serving as consul in 59 BC, Caesar was ordered by the Senate to assume command in Illyria and Cisalpine Gaul and, shortly afterwards, in Narbonese Gaul also. In the March of 58 he began his wars of conquest in Gaul, which were effectively completed by 50 BC, with the fall of Alesia and the capture of the Arvernian warlord Vercingetorix.

Tempted by the riches of the country, and keen to increase his influence at home, Caesar was looking for an excuse to invade free Gaul, and he found it in the intended migration of the Helvetii, a Celtic nation. They were moving westwards in search of new lands, and to do this they needed to pass through Roman controlled territory. Caesar refused their request for free passage, and barred their way near Geneva. When the Helvetii then turned north, into the tribal lands of the Sequani, Caesar pursued them, and laid siege to Bibracte, the capital of the Aedui. After gaining a decisive victory, he forced the remainder of the Helvetii to retreat into what is modern day western Switzerland.

Next, Caesar moved against the German warlord Ariovistus, who had invaded the lands of the Sequani, and drove him and his nation back across the Rhine. In the following year, 57 BC, he won crushing victories over the Nervii and Eburones of northern Gaul, and in 56 he moved up the Atlantic coast to the Channel, conquering the Veneti, the Menapians and the Morini - three tribes which carried on extensive trade with Britain.

Caesar owed his success not only to his abilities as a general, but also to his outstanding diplomatic skills, which enabled him to play off one Celtic tribe against another, to his own personal advantage. His careful choice of allies benefited him greatly, too.

With great foresight, he had made a friendly chieftain, Commius, king of the Gallic Atrebates. While

Fig.25. Atrebates/Gaul, silver unit, 14mm.
DLT 8682.
Romanised horse right. COMMIOS.
H. De La Tour, Atlas de Monnaies Gauloises, Pt. XXXV, 8682.

Caesar was planning his first expedition to Britain, Commius helped him to gain influence among the British Atrebates, and to convince them of the advantages of an alliance with Rome (**Gallic War** 4, 21).

By the winter of 56-55 BC, Caesar regarded his conquest of Gaul as largely complete, but he had greatly underestimated the passion for freedom among the defeated tribes, and failed to foresee their decision to unite and continue the fight against their oppressors. He could not even rely on the loyalty of his protégé Commius. In the winter of 54-53 fresh revolts broke out in Gaul, under the general leadership of Vercingetorix - a revolt in which Commius and his Atrebates joined. When Vercingetorix's Gallic alliance was finally destroyed, and he was put to death in Rome six years later, Commius made good his escape to Britain. Here he founded a dynasty that lasted until the later Claudian invasion.

In 56 BC the end of Caesar's five-year governorship was approaching. In order to protect his position at home - particularly with regard to his great rival Pompey - he asked the Senate for an extension of his appointment, and especially requested its approval of his policies in Gaul. As Caesar particularly wanted to avoid his planned invasion of Britain being seen as a war of aggression, it was very convenient for him that a young Trinovantian prince, Mandubracius by name, should come to him for asylum. His tribe, which inhabited present day Suffolk, had been attacked by the Catuvellauni under their king, Cassivellaunus. His father had been driven out or killed, his lands seized, and the capital, Camulodunum, occupied. Caesar granted this plea for help, and placed Mandubracius and his people under the protection of Rome. Hostages were demanded from the Catuvellauni, and corn supplies were to be sent over for the Roman army. Cassivellaunus was sternly warned by Caesar "not to make any trouble for Mandubracius and the Trinovantes" (**Gallic War** 5, 22).

Other reasons behind Caesar's invasion of Britain were the help and support the island Celts had been giving to their Gaulish neighbours, and also the enticing reports brought back by Gaulish merchants. Britain, they said, was brimming with resources, rich in treasures such as gold and pearls, and an abundant source of slaves.[5.]

Before the invasion began, Caesar had British merchants and inhabitants closely questioned about the political and military situation in Britain, and also about the islanders' readiness for war. His ally Commius found suitable landing beaches for the fleet, and negotiated alliances, or at least neutrality, with individual tribes.

In Gaul, Caesar took precautions for his absence. Above all, Dumnorix, chief of the Aedui, was the wild card. In order to keep open his retreat, and to avoid any disturbances while he was away, Dumnorix was ordered to accompany the expedition. When the latter refused to go, Caesar had him put to death on the spot. As he was being bound, he shouted out, proud and defiant, that he was a free man, and the son of a free people. (**Gallic War** 5,7).

In spite of all Caesar's efforts, this, his first invasion of Britain with two legions, undertaken in the late summer of 55 BC, seems to modern eyes to have been poorly organised.

The expedition was not a great success. On reaching the British coast, the legionaries had great trouble disembarking, because of the rough seas. The Britons knew they were coming, and were waiting for them, lined up on the coast in battle array. The tactics of the Britons were new to Caesar, and were hard to deal with – they mounted their attacks from chariots, a means of war long since abandoned in Gaul.

Although he had gained a partial success, Caesar soon realised that with no cavalry he was leading his army into danger, and he sought for a means of leaving the island as soon as possible. Frequent storms were making the flow of reinforcements and supplies impossible.

Fig.26. Aedui/Gaul, Dumnorix, silver unit, 16mm. Time of Caesar.
DLT 5044.
DVBNOCOV.
Warrior with head of enemy. Carnyx in front of warrior.
Cabinet de médailles, Paris.

Fig.27. Roman Republic, L. Hostilius Saserna, denarius, 19mm, 49 BC.
Head of Vercingetorix.
Celtic warrior in war chariot.
Tkalek AG, Zürich, 2001, 231,

A minor victory over his opponents allowed Caesar to avoid loss of face. He took hostages, and returned to Gaul. This failed attempt is dressed up by Caesar in his **Gallic War** as having been nothing more than a reconnaissance of the island, just "a quick look round" in order to "assess the kind of people living there, and to study the country, its harbours and their approaches" (**Gallic War** 4,20.). His report to the Senate was so skilfully worded that an unusually long *supplicatio* (thanksgiving for success) was ordered, a festival twenty days long, in order to celebrate his success and "victory". (**Gallic War** 4, 38).

Caesar's next attempt took place the following year, and was far better prepared. He set out in flat-bottomed ships, this time with five legions and two thousand cavalry. Faced by this menace, the British tribes buried their rivalries, and placed overall command in the hands of Cassivellaunus. Direct confrontation, a pitched battle against the superior Roman troops, was something that the Celtic general preferred to avoid. Instead, he adopted a form of guerrilla warfare, attacking rear areas and making good use of his knowledge of the country. But after a few skirmishes, rivalries between the tribes broke out afresh, and Caesar was able to make good use of this to force a peace. He imposed tribute, which the Britons were to pay annually to Rome, but it is far from clear how long this tribute was paid, or indeed whether it was ever paid at all. However, a hoard of about two thousand gold coins discovered at Whaddon, a village near Milton Keynes, in Buckinghamshire, and dating between 50 and 40 BC, may well have been intended to be the first instalment of Rome's tribute.

Caesar, having briefly crossed the Thames and reached Verulamium (St. Albans), caused the Romans to regard all southern Britain from then on as being within their sphere of influence. Caesar's expedition was a turning point – it marks the entry of Britain into history.

Fig.28. Catuvellauni gold stater, Whaddon Chase type. 22mm, c.55-45 BC.
VA 1493.
Abstracted head of Apollo right.
Romanised horse right, sunflower below horse.
Lanz, München 68, June 1994, 3.

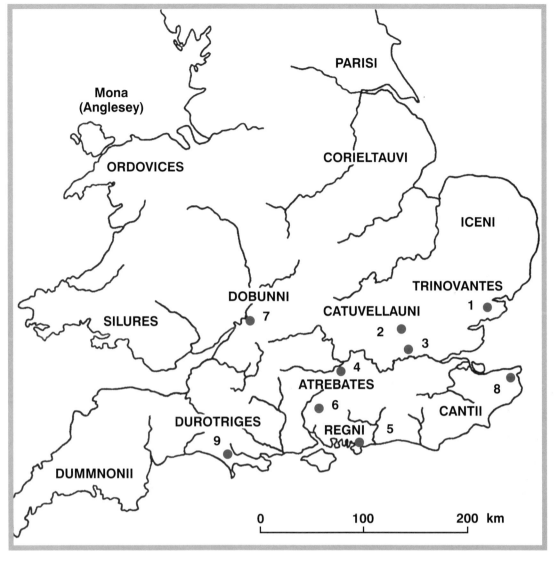

Southern Britain, showing the principal tribes and towns.
After Philip de Jersey, "Celtic Coinage in Britain", London 2001.

1. Camulodunum (Colchester)

2. Verulamium (St. Albans)

3. Londinium (London)

4. Calleva (Silchester)

5. Noviomagus (Chichester)

6. Venta Belgarum (Winchester)

7. Glevum (Gloucester)

8. Rutupiae (Richborough)

9. Durnovaria (Dorchester).

The Celtic Tribes Of Britain
& Early Celtic Coinage

The question of when Britain was first settled by Celtic speaking peoples is very difficult to answer. New research seems to suggest a first wave of immigrants in the 5th century BC, followed later in the century by further groups. In about 75 BC the southern part of the island was invaded by Belgic tribes from northern Gaul "in order to seize plunder and make war" (**Gallic War** 5, 12). Caesar tells us that these new arrivals quickly made themselves at home in Britain, but yet retained their old tribal names. This explains why we find tribes such as the Atrebates and Parisi on both sides of the Channel.

The Atrebates

The Atrebates, along with the Catuvellauni and Trinovantes, were, in the late 1st century BC and the early 1st century AD, among the most important and powerful tribes of Britain. Their capital was at Calleva, present day Silchester. They had formed a tribal alliance with their neighbours to the south, the Regni or Regnenses, who occupied the area around Noviomagus (Chichester).

The first coinage of the Atrebates and Regni, dating from about 75 BC, is the gold of the so-called "Westerham Type", which in numismatic literature is often assigned to the Trinovantes. Along with the lighter "Atrebatic Abstract" type, they were in circulation during the Gallic Wars.[6.] On the Westerham-B Type, one of the best executed examples of early Celtic coin art in Britain, only the laurel wreath is recognisable of the portrait on the original, while on

the reverse the horse and charioteer are reduced merely to a pattern of crescents and dots.

However, the style had changed completely by 55-45 BC, when a quarter stater appeared, an absolute masterpiece of Celtic art and of great religious symbolism. The strictly symmetrical obverse shows two wheels, the attributes of Taranis, the god of heaven, between two plaited bands and with decoration above and below. The reverse again shows a wheel, above a relatively realistic horse. The bird between the legs of the horse may be an eagle, the symbol of Taranis, or a raven, the sign of Teutates. It may even represent Lug, or some local war god - we cannot be sure. The three-ended tail of the horse, like the three wheels on the coin, represents a threefold deity or Trinity, or alternatively the three various aspects of one single god.

Fig.29. Trinovantes, gold stater, Westerham B or Clacton type.
18mm, c.65-55 BC.
VA 1458; dJ 21 var.
Abstract head of Apollo right.
Disjointed horse left.
Chris Rudd, list 54, 2000, 71.

Fig.30. Atrebates gold stater, Atrebatic Abstract (British Q) type
18mm, 55-45 BC.
VA 212; dJ 32
Apollo head variant.
Horse with triple tail right,
eight-spoked wheel below horse.
Chris Rudd, list 69, 2003, no.16.

Fig.31. Atrebates gold quarter stater, 13mm, c.55-45 BC.
VA 236.
Apollo head variant.
Celticised horse with triple tail left, bird below horse,
eight-spoked wheel above horse.
Chris Rudd, list 54, 2000, 15.

Fig.32. Atrebates, Commius, gold stater, 16mm, c.45-30 BC.
VA 350; dJ 36.
Celticised head of Apollo right.
Celtic horse right, five-spoked wheel.
[CO]MMIOS.
Chris Rudd list 54, 2000, V 350.

Dynastic coinage among the Atrebates begins with Commius in about 50 to 40 BC, although a dating of 45 to 30 has also been suggested. A stater struck in about 45 BC differs from the earlier "Atrebatic Abstract Type" only by the name COMMIOS. A quarter stater with a monogram (digamma, A or AT) on the obverse, and a horse on the reverse is attributed to Commius, as are silver units, bearing on the obverse a severely stylised head and a double spiral, and on the reverse again a horse.

Fig.33. Atrebates, Commius, gold quarter stater,
Anemone type. 9mm, c.45-30 BC.
VA 353.
Digamma on blank field.
Horse left, "anemone" above horse.
Leu AG, Zürich 86, 2003,
Chris Rudd list 63, 2002, 26.

Fig.34. Atrebates, Commius, silver unit, 12mm, c.45-30 BC.
VA 355-5.
Celticised head left, two pellet-in-ring motifs in front of face.
Celticised horse left.
Chris Rudd, list 54, 2000, no.16.

The Cantii

Caesar mentions the inhabitants of Cantium, modern day Kent, as being the most civilised. He regarded all other Britons as no more than savages - dressed in animal skins, with long hair and covered in blue paint - which gave them a terrifying appearance in battle (**Gallic War** 5, 14).

The striking of coins began among the Cantii as early as about 100 BC, or perhaps even earlier still. Their cast bronze and potin coins went through frequent variations and stages of development until they were discontinued in about 35 BC. The designs of their obverses and reverses are greatly simplified, and their importance is much reduced. Just a few lines and simple strokes represent a head in profile, or a bull, the horns of which are suggested by crescent patterns.[7.]

Fig.35. Cantii, cast bronze, Angular Bull type.
17mm, c.85-50 BC.
VA 133.
Abstract head of Apollo left.
Celticised bull charging left.
R. Pudill

Fig.36. Cantii, gold quarter stater, Early Trophy type.
11mm, c.45-40 BC.
VA 146; dJ 35.
Blank.
Trophy still recognisable; two rings and boxes with
cross-hatching.
Leu AG, Zürich 86, May 2003, 2.

Fig.37. Caesar, denarius, 19mm, c.50 BC.
Seaby I Caesar 18; BMC 3955.
Head of Pietas or Venus right.
Trophy of Gallic arms. Gallic shield and axe.
Dannheimer, Gebhard, Das kelt. Jahrtausend Abb. 196.

A quarter stater with a blank obverse and a stylised trophy on the reverse, is also attributed to the Cantii. These were probably copied from the *denarii* of Caesar, with the Gallic Victory type.[8] The silver unit of "Facing Heads" type can also be assigned to them - two clean-shaven male heads facing one another with the horns of a ram between them. If the coin is turned through 180 degrees, then Teutates, the horned god, is seen.[9] The practice of relating the designs of obverse and reverse (*nummus conversus*), with which we in more modern times are familiar (for example the satirical medallions of the 16th century, showing Pope and Devil, or Cardinal and Fool) were popular with the Celts. They loved *trompe l'oeil* effects, hidden faces, and hidden meanings on their coins.

Fig.38. Cantii, silver unit, Facing Head type. 12mm,
c.50-30 BC.
Facing heads.
Celticised horse left.
Leu AG, Zürich 86, May 2003, 3.
Chris Rudd list 27, 1997, 22.

Hidden faces on Celtic coins.
Chris Rudd list 29, 1997, 74.

An example of a hidden face on the obverse of a
gold stater of Tasciovanus, (VA 1732-5).

An issue of gold staters in about 50-40 BC, with a fishing net type design, similar to those of the Gaulish Parisi, gave rise to the name "Weald Fishing Net". It is, however, far from certain whether a fishing net really is intended, or whether this is simply an ornamental pattern. However, fishing was unquestionably a great source of protein in the Celtic diet.

Fig.39. Cantii, gold stater, "Fishing Net" or early Weald type. 17mm, c.50-40BC.
VA144.
Plain.
Celticised horse left,
"Fishing net" below horse.
Chris Rudd list 54, 2000, 12.

The Belgae

The lands of the Belgae, comprising present day Wiltshire and Hampshire, lay to the west of the Atrebates and Regni. Their capital was at Venta Belgarum (Winchester).

Of the history of this tribe, very little information has come down to us. It cannot be ruled out, however, that fairly early on the Belgae emigrated, or simply amalgamated with another tribe.

Except for imported Gallo-Belgic types, there are only a few early and very rare examples of Belgic coinage, as for example the "Sun and Moons" or the "Kingsclere Horse Box Type". The so-called dynastic coinages of the Belgae have long since been dismissed as fantasy.

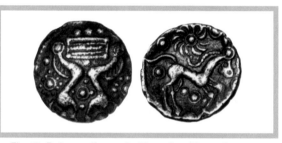

Fig.40. Belgae, silver unit, Kingsclere Horse Box type.
14mm, c.50-40BC.
Box with hatching between two animals (?).
Celticised horse right,
12-armed spiral above horse.
Chris Rudd list 54, 2000, 33.

The Durotriges

The territory of the Durotriges included present day Dorset and the southern part of Somerset. Quite close to their capital, Durnovaria (Dorchester), stood the most famous hill-fort in Britain, Maiden Castle. Archaeology has shown that this *oppidum*, defended by several rings of banks and ditches, was not only a political and economic capital, but at the same time an important centre of Iron Age religion. During the Roman invasion, this fortress was taken by storm by the future emperor Vespasian and his Legion II Augusta, during their march through western Britain. (Clayton 185f.).

Fig.41. Durotriges, silver stater, Abstract type. 20mm, c.58-45 BC.
VA 1235 var; dJ 71 var.
Abstract head of Apollo right.
Cranborne Chase type. Disjointed horse left.
Chris Rudd, list 27, 1997, no.83.

The early staters of the Durotriges are similar to those of the Trinovantes. However, they preferred to strike in silver, as for example the "Cranborne Chase Type", issued from about 58 to 45 BC. The obverses show only a few traces of the original head, such as stylised curls, a wreath cut through with a diagonal line which indicated the face and nose, and crescents for the lips and eyes. The horse on the reverse has also been greatly simplified. Its legs look like dumb-bells, its mane and charioteer are indicated by just dots, and its body is simply made up of just crescents. On well-struck examples, one can still make out the three-ended tail. Later examples of this type are struck in billon, a copper-zinc alloy containing little more than a trace of silver.

Fig 42: Durotriges, potin (cast bronze), Hengistbury Seven-Seven-Ten type. 16mm, c.AD 10-45.
VA 1344/45; dJ 72.
Only a large Y remains of the head of Apollo.
Ten pellets in field.
Leu AG, Zürich 86, 2003, 38.

A further simplification - and the final stage in a long process of reduction and stylisation from the Greek original - was the "Hengistbury Six-Six-Ten Type". This was a cast bronze coin, which circulated throughout the tribal lands of the Durotriges from about 40 BC until the close of Celtic coin production in England. The invariable design is six circles either side of an epsilon to indicate a head, and ten more for the horse and charioteer.

Departing from the usual head and horse design, and with far more obscure meanings, are the "Geometric Type" or "Duro Boat Bird" gold and silver, struck in about 50 to 30 BC. The obverse is generally described as "Three Men in a Boat", and the reverse as "Lightning and Bird".

Fig.43. Durotriges, silver unit, Late-Geometric type.
11mm, c.58-45 BC.
VA 1242; dJ 73.
"Three men in a boat".
Vertically-oriented zigzag across field. Y-like object on either side of zigzag.
R. Pudill

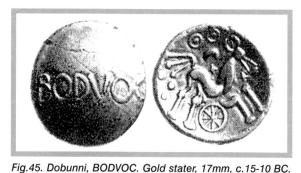

Fig.44. Dobunni EISV. Gold stater, 18mm, c.AD 15-30.
VA 1105; dJ 69.
Tree-like object.
Celticised horse right; tail has three strands with pellet
finiels. EISV above horse.
Chris Rudd, list 66, 2002, no.59.

Fig.45. Dobunni, BODVOC. Gold stater, 17mm, c.15-10 BC.
VA 1052; dJ65.
BODVOC
Celticised horse right; tail has three strands with pellet
finiels. Eight-spoked wheel below horse.
Wacher 1979.

The Dobunni

The lands of the Dobunni, with their capital at Bagendon, near Corinium (Cirencester), included the Mendip and Cotswold Hills, as well as parts of present day Herefordshire and Worcestershire. They were bounded by the lands of the Durotriges and Belgae to the south, and the Catuvellauni to the east.

The coins of this tribe bear what are probably the names of rulers in abbreviated form, such as CORIO-, BODVOC-, ANTED-, COMVX-, EISV- and CATTI- (Birley, People 23). Metrological and metallurgic experiments have allowed us to give an approximate dating of 30 to 10 BC for the kings from Corio- to Comux-. Eisu- and Catti- appear to have struck in about AD 43, the date of the Claudian invasion. (VA 266 f).

The principal characteristic of Dobunnic gold is a branch or tree-like object, possibly a totem of the tribe, or a dynastic symbol.[10.] On the reverses of the staters there generally appear the horse with the triple tail, and the sun-wheel of Taranis, the god of heaven.

Fig.46. Berkshire, silver unit, 14mm, c.55-45 BC. Abingdon
Head type, Num. Circ. May 1998, 1.150.
Celticised head left; crescents for hair.
Celticised horse right, small horses (?) above and below.
Chris Rudd, list 81, 2005, no.31.

Dobunnic silver of the second half of the 1st century BC shows a stylised head, sometimes with a moonlike face, and with three or four crescents for hair. Above and below the horse on the reverse the space is filled by either the head of a bird, another horse, as in the illustration, or else the head of a cockerel (The "Cotswold Cock" type).[11.]

The Corieltauvi

The Corieltauvi, (previously thought to have been called Coritani), occupied the East Midlands, approximately the modern counties of Nottinghamshire, Leicestershire and Lincolnshire. They had their capital at Ratae, present day Leicester.

Among the early coins of the Corieltauvi we can distinguish two main groups. The "North East Coast" type, deriving from the "Abstract Design" type of the Ambiani, and the "South Ferriby" type, previously attributed to the Brigantes. This last has a style all its own, which is impossible to mistake. The obverse is often blank, or has an abstract head, rather like the "Cranborne Chase" types of the Durotriges. On the reverse is a horse, whose neck, body and tail are formed by three or five semi-circular shapes, in a

Fig.47. Corieltauvi, gold stater, South-Ferriby type.
18mm, c.45-10 BC.
VA 811.
Blank.
Disjointed horse left, seven-pointed star below horse.
R. Pudill

Fig.48. Corieltauvi, silver unit, Hosidius type.
16mm, c.55-45 BC.
VA 855.
Spear pierces boar's back; elaborate "anemone" above boar.
Celticised horse left; large ring of pellets
with central pellet above horse.
Triton I, Zürich 1997, 2200.

most startling design, and the head is simply a square. Between its dumbbell-like legs a star appears, symbolising the sun.

A noteworthy issue among the anepigraphic coins of the Corieltauvi is the "Hosidius" type, appearing in about 55 to 45 BC. On the obverse is a long legged boar, with hackles raised on its neck and back, pierced by a spear. In the upper left field is a carefully detailed solar "Anemone", and above the head of the boar is a swastika. The reverse is decorated with circular symbols above and beneath a horse, whose tail is divided into chevron like shapes.

Like the Dobunni, the Corieltauvi began to put named inscriptions on their coins at the end of the 1st century BC. Here again, we can say with certainty that these are either shortened forms or abbreviations of the names of kings, for example: VEP-, VEP-COR- F (this may mean Vep-, son of Cor-) or VEPO-CO-, AVN- AST- or AVN- COST-, DVMNOC-TIGIR- or DVMNOC- TIGIR- SENO-, VOLISIOS DVMNOVELLAVNOS or DVMNOCOVEROS or VOLISIOS CARTIVELLAVNOS. Vep- or Vepo- are in our opinion abbreviations of Vepogeni or Vepogenos, which may be translated as "Child of Weapons" (Birkhan 423).

Fig.49. Corieltauvi, DVMNOC TIGIR SENO. Gold stater,
17mm, c.AD 15-20.
VA 972; dJ 78.
Apollo-Wreath; DV and M[N] between lines to left and
right.
Celticised horse left. TIGIR above horse,
[SE]NO below horse.
CNG 57, April 2001, 1734.

Fig.50. Corieltauvi, VOLISIOS DVMNO COVEROS. Gold
stater, 19mm, c.AD 20-35.
VA 978.
Apollo-Wreath. VO LI SI OS between lines.
[D]VMNOCO V[EROS] around Celticised horse.
Chris Rudd, list 20, 1995, no.16.

The Iceni Or Eceni

The Iceni, or Eceni, of present day Norfolk, enter the spotlight of history with the revolt of Boudica against the tyranny of the Roman occupiers in AD 60. Their coinage begins with the "Norfolk Wolf" type gold stater in about 65 BC, followed by the "Freckenham" types of about 45 to 40 BC. The design referred to in numismatic literature as the "Freckenham Flower Type" is more likely to be a symbol of the threefold god of heaven, or of the three aspects of this one single deity.[12.]

Fig.51. Iceni, gold stater, 17mm, c.65-45 BC.
VA 610.
Abstract head of Apollo right.
Norfolk Wolf type. Wolf left.
Chris Rudd, list 58, 2001, no.33.

Fig.52. Iceni, gold stater, Freckenham Flower type.
17mm, c.45-40 BC.
VA 626.
Floral pattern.
Celticised horse right; large outline crescent decorated with zigzag line and pellets.
Chris Rudd list 53, 2000, 39.

Fig.53. Iceni, gold stater, Freckenham type.
16mm, c.45-40 BC.
VA 626; dJ 80.
Floral pattern.
Celticised horse right, wheels above and below.
Chris Rudd list 53, 2000, 49.

This gold quarter stater of the Irstead type, struck between about 30 and 10 BC, shows a trellis pattern in the centre, surrounded by ornamental decorations.

This silver coin of the Iceni is referred to by the name of "Odin's Eye", on account of the head's over-sized and apparently blind eye.

Fig.54. Iceni, gold quarter stater, Late Freckenham or Irstead type. 10mm, 45-40 BC.
VA 628.
Box consisting of lines in centre, branches wreaths at sides of box.
Celticised horse right; trefoil above horse.
Triton II, Zürich 1998, 1226.

Fig.55. Iceni, silver unit, Odin's Eye type. 14mm, c.20-15 BC.
VA 665.
Celticised head right with "dead eye".
Celticised horse right, spoked wheel and ring-pellet motif above and below .
Chris Rudd list 54, 2000, 42.

Fig.56. Iceni, CAN DVRO. Silver unit, Boar type. 1
3mm, c.25-20 BC.
VA 663.
Celticised boar right.
Celticised horse right, CAN above, DVRO below horse.
CNG 57, 2001, 1754.

Whether this silver unit, with the inscription CAN- DVRO- appeared in 25 to 20 BC, or belongs to the so-called dynastic issues of the early 1st century AD, is uncertain.

Fig.57. Iceni silver unit, Bury type. 14mm, c.40-50 BC.
dJ 82.
Head of Andraste (?) with intricate diadem and numerous
decorative motifs right.
Naturalistic horse right, solar rosette above horse.
Chris Rudd, list 15, 1995, no.26.

This coin, with a female head wearing a carefully detailed diadem ("Diadem Type" or "Bury Diadem") dismissed as "imported" by Van Arsdell, is nowadays attributed to the Iceni. It is a silver unit, struck probably between 50 and 40 BC. This may well be a portrait of the Celtic war goddess Andraste, of whom, as we have seen, Boudica was an ardent worshipper.[13] On better preserved examples a ram-headed serpent, the sign of Teutates or Dispater, is to be seen before the face of Andraste. On the reverse is a horse, and above it the sun-wheel, or else the sun itself, with dumbbell-shaped rays.

Fig.58. Iceni silver unit, Face Horse type or "Boudica".
14mm, c.20-15 BC.
VA "Boudica" 792; dJ 83.
Celticised head right.
Celticised horse right, large, elaborate wheel-like object
above horse.
Chris Rudd, list 40, 1999, no.15.

It is important not to place too much importance on the distribution of finds, because this can be very misleading when attributing a particular coin to a particular time or place. A good example of this is the silver unit which Van Arsdell attributed to Queen Boudica. There is a great deal of evidence, principally in its style, for giving this issue a much earlier date. It is strange, too, that there should have been this large issue of uninscribed coins, when for some time now Icenian coins had been almost invariably inscribed.[14]

Fig 59: Iceni, ANTED. Silver unit, 13mm, c.AD 1-25.
VA 715.
Double crescent emblem.
Celticised horse right. Rosette above and three pellets below
horse. Monogram below horse simplified to the letter T.
Chris Rudd, list 47, 1999, no.41.

Fig.60. Iceni, AESV. Silver unit, 13mm, c.AD 50-55.
VA 770; dJ 87.
Double crescent emblem.
Celticised horse right. AESV below horse.
Chris Rudd, list 70, 2003, no.44.

Fig.61. Iceni, AESV. Silver unit, 13mm, c.AD 55-60.
VA 775.
Double crescent emblem.
Celticised horse right. AESV below horse.
Chris Rudd, list 80, 2005, no.39.

The dynastic coinages of the Iceni contain short-ened forms, or abbreviations, of the names of kings such as ANTED (IOS?), SAENV (SIOS?) and AESV (BILINOS?). The name Saenusios is echoed in the tribal name S(a)enius, which is found in Britain after the Claudian conquest, and Aesu(bilinos) may derive from the Celtic god Esus. Interestingly, in Colchester a shrine to Esus has been found, dedicated by a freedman called Aesubilinus, perhaps a descendant or relative of the Icenian ruler (Birley, People 24 et seq.).

The inscriptions ECE- and ECEN-, which occur on the coinage from about AD 25 may perhaps be shortened versions of a personal name such as Ecen(ios?), but generally these are regarded as being more likely abbreviations of the tribal name.

The dynastic coinages of the Iceni close with Pra-sutagus, who will be discussed in more detail later.

Great difficulty is presented by the dating and interpretation of a rare silver coin bearing the inscription ALE- SCA-, which Van Arsdell has attrib-uted to the Corieltauvi, and which de Jersey gives to the Iceni. Various pointers incline us to place it late in the reign of Prasutagus.

Fig.62. Iceni, ECEN. Silver unit, Ecen Tribal type.
14mm, c.AD 25-38.
VA 730; dJ 86 var.
Double crescent emblem.
[E]CEN, Celticised horse right.
Chris Rudd, list 53, 2000, 55.

Fig 63: Iceni, ALE SCA. Silver unit, 13 mm,
c.10 BC-AD 10 (?).
VA 996 (Cor.).
Boar right, pellet-in-ring motifs. ALE.
Celticised horse right. SCA below horse.
Chris Rudd list 54, 2000, 48.

The Catuvellauni & The Trinovantes

The tribe of the Catuvellauni, with their capital at Verulamium, Verolamion, or Verlamio (St Albans), and their neighbours to the east, the Trinovantes, were united under Cunobelin (circa AD 10-43). As the capital of his new empire, this son of Tasciovanus (as he styles himself on his coins) chose Camulodunum (Colchester), which means "fortress of Camulos", the war god.

Attributing the early, anepigraphic coins to the Catuvellauni or Trinovantes is far from easy, which is why Van Arsdell and De Jersey treat them jointly as "North Thames coinage"[15.] Among these issues are the "Clacton" type, and also the "Whaddon Chase" type of circa 50-40 BC, previously mentioned in connexion with the tribute payments. John Sills suggests that: "Westerham" type gold staters were struck north and south of the Thames by Cassivellaunus to finance the British campaign against Caesar in 54 BC (see Chris Rudd list 27, 1997, 2-5, and list 33, 1998, 2-4).

A small silver coin of the Catuvellauni, struck in about 50 BC, and a quarter stater, show on their reverse a horse, very similar in style to the Whaddon Chase type.

The obverses, however, particularly that of the silver coin, are very different, both in design and style. On the extremely rare "Amersham Moon Man Type" appears the clean-shaven head of a young man. From his hairline, represented by three crescents, his hair streams out in braided tufts, giving him a demonic appearance. On the reverse, above the usual horse with the threefold tail, there is a rosette, representing the sun, and between the legs of the horse there is a palm branch.

On the "Finney's Thunderbolt" quarter stater there are two braided bands, in the shape of a lightning flash, bending twice at right angles. On either side of it is a circle of dots. On the reverse is a horse, with symbolic suns above and below.

Fig.64. Catuvellauni gold stater, Middle Whaddon Chase type. 16mm, c.45-40 BC.
VA 1487; dJ 30 var.
Crossing wreaths.
Romanised horse right; wing-like object above horse, six-spoked wheel below horse.
Chris Rudd, list 72, 2003, no.60.

Fig.65. Catuvellauni silver unit, Amersham Moon Man type. 12mm, c.45-40 BC.
Coiled hair, hair appendage formed by crescents.
Celticised horse left.
Leu AG, Zürich 86, 2003, 42.
Chris Rudd list 59, 2001, 60.

Fig.66. Catuvellauni gold quarter stater, Finney's Thunderbolt type. 11mm, c.55-45 BC.
Similar VA 1478.
Spike made up of line and pellets, two pellet-in-ring motifs.
Romanised horse right.
Leu AG, Zürich 86, 2003, 42.
Chris Rudd list 60, 2002, 63,

Fig.67. Trinovantes in Essex, Addedomaros. Gold stater,
17mm, 40-37 BC.
VA 1605 (first coinage).
Crossed wreaths.
Romanised horse wheel under horse. ADDEOMA.
Lanz, München 68, June 1994, 4.

Fig.68. Trinovantes, Addedomaros. (second coinage).
Gold stater, 16mm, 37-33 BC.
VA 1620; dJ 50.
Six-armed spiral.
Spiral type. Romanised horse, cornucopiae or harp
below horse. [ADDIIDOM] above horse.
Chris Rudd, list 69, 2003, no.55.

After Mandubracius, who sought help from Caesar, Addedomaros, circa 40-20 BC, is the first leader of the Trinovantes whose name is known to us. His early gold staters with the inscription ADDEDI-IDOM-, ADDIIDOM-, or AØØEDMA- are reminiscent of the Whaddon Chase type. His "Spiral" type, struck from about 35 BC shows on the obverse a six-armed figure, vaguely resembling a starfish.

In the last year of Addedomaros' reign, Tasciovanus (circa 20-10 BC) rose to power among the Catuvellauni, the Trinovantes western neighbours. On his coins, struck at Verulamium, otherwise Verlamio (St Albans), this king titles himself RICON (king), the Celtic form of rex, in order to distance himself from Rome, and to show an unwelcoming attitude to her growing influence in Celtic Britain.[16]

Fig.69. Catuvellauni, Tasciovanus (third coinage).
Gold stater, 17mm, 15-10 BC.
VA 1780; dJ 55.
Inscription on vertical wreath: TASCIO RICON
Celtic warrior on horse left, pellet-in-ring motif below horse.
Chris Rudd, list 78, 2004, no.53.

Fig.70. Catuvellauni, Tasciovanus (first coinage.) Gold
quarter stater, 12mm, 25-20 BC.
VA 1692.
Crossed wreaths. Inscription: T A [S C] in angles.
Celtic warrior on horse right, AS from TASC below horse.
R. Pudill

The early coinages of Tasciovanus are reminiscent of the "Whaddon Chase" types, which generally have a *bucranium*, or bull's head, above the horse. The obverses have symmetrical and finely detailed patterns, which are usually described as "crossed wreaths". If the design is studied carefully for a while, then faces seem to appear, which immediately disappear as soon as one thinks one sees them clearly. The Celts seem to have loved these "hidden faces", similar in a way to the *trompe l'oeil* pictures of today, which speaks of their delight in anything surreal, dreamlike, or mysterious, and also for their sense of humour.

Fig.71. Catuvellauni, Tasciovanus. (second coinage).
Gold stater, 18mm, 20-15 BC.
Crossed wreaths. Two hidden faces.
Celticised horse right, bucranium above and bird (?)
below horse.
Leu AG, Zürich 33, 1983, 164.

Stone relief of a three-faced god from Soissons, France.
The beards are made up of corn ears. On the base
(out of the photograph) are a ram and a cock, creatures
sacred to Mercury. This is therefore most likely
to be a representation of Teutates.

This hidden face is echoed by a stone relief of a bearded, three-faced god at Soissons in France, where the images seem to disappear and reappear somewhere else. This elusiveness, this inability to imagine how their gods really looked, says much about the Celts' attitude to their religion, because it was only under the influence of Rome that Celtic gods first became finite beings, and by degrees assumed human form. That said, it appears that the Celts never stopped seeing them as omnipresent and indefinable.[17.]

Tasciovanus' second issue of gold is marked by an important change. The usual Celtic horse gives way to a horseman. The coins show either a warrior at full gallop, with turned head, as though being pursued by some enemy, or else a rider with a carnyx, a Celtic war trumpet. The bell-mouth of this characteristically Celtic instrument was usually in the shape of a boar, as appears on the Gundestrup cauldron.[18.] Valuable information is provided about the weapons and equipment of Celtic warriors both by this find, from the peat bogs of Jutland, and the gold staters of Tasciovanus. Together, these two sources confirm many points contained in a 1st century account by Diodorus Siculus.[19.]

Horsemen brandishing carnyx.

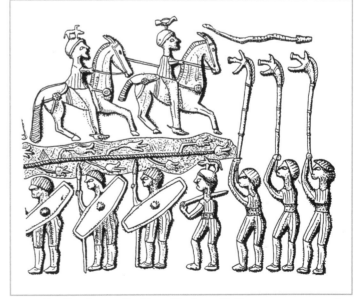

The Gundestrup Cauldron. Warriors with Carnyces, some wearing
helmets decorated with animals, carrying a sacred tree.
Copenhagen, Nationalmuseet.

Fig.72. Catuvellauni, Tasciovanus (third coinage). Silver
unit, 14mm, 15-10 BC.
VA 1800.
TASC in tablet.
Celtic warrior with elliptical shield left.
R. Pudill.

Fig.73. Roman Republic, Albinus Bruti F. denarius,
18mm. 49-48 BC.
Syd. 941 var.
Bust of Mars
Albinus Bruti. Gallic weapons and carnyx.
Tkalek AG, Zürich, 2001, 233.

The basic equipment of the Celtic fighting man was simply a spear and shield. The better-heeled warrior also had a helmet and sword and - later on - armour, or a mail tunic of iron. Finds indicate that their spears were unusually long. Their wooden shields were leather covered, and gaudily painted according to the owner's taste. These were of an impressive size, up to one and a half metres high, and their shapes varied: some were elongated ovals, others square with rounded corners, and yet others six-sided or even lozenge-shaped, as is apparent from a silver unit of Tasciovanus. Round shields were also known.

Diodorus has left us an account of Celtic helmets, frequently decorated with extravagant crests. Such items may have had religious significance, or else proclaimed the status of the wearer. Typical features of the early iron helmets of the Gauls, from the 4th century BC onwards, were the pronounced point, and the integral neck protection. During the following century cheek plates were added, an idea borrowed from Italy. In the middle of the 1st century BC new models came into fashion, notably the "ridged bowler style", appearing on a gold stater of Tasciovanus (James 76f).

Fig.74. Catuvellauni, Tasciovanus (second coinage). Gold
stater, 17mm. 20-15 BC.
VA 1732-9.
Crossed wreaths, two hidden faces.
Celtic warrior on horse right.
R. Pudill.

Fig 75: Catuvellauni, Tasciovanus.
Gold stater, 17mm, 20-15 BC.
VA 1730-5.
Reverse Celtic warrior on horse right.
Chris Rudd, list 20, 1995.

The "ridged Bowler" helmet.

Celtic Helmets. R.M. Weiss, "Ein reiches Kriegsgrab aus Magdalenska Gora". In: Acta Praehistorica 28, 1996, 40-58.

The style of the horseman on this coin demonstrates particularly well the relationship between Celtic and so-called modern art, as a comparison with one of Picasso's drawings will show.[20.]

The mail shirt, with its thousands of interlocking rings, and a masterpiece of the blacksmith's art, was probably a Celtic invention. The earliest finds are from burials of the 3rd century BC. Mail was an extremely valuable possession, and would have been handed down from one generation of warriors to the next. One such piece is clearly shown on a gold coin of TASCIO(VANVS) RICON.

*Pablo Picasso: Paseo de cuadrillas (detail).
Entry of the bullfighters into the Arena. Cannes, 1957.
Compare to a gold stater of Tasciovanus
(Tkalec, AG, Zürich, 2002, Nr. 5.).*

*Fig.76. Catuvellauni, Tasciovanus (third coinage).
Gold stater, 17mm, 15-10 BC.
VA1780-5; dJ 55.
Inscription on vertical wreath: TASCIO RICON.
Celtic warrior wearing chain mail on horse left.
Chris Rudd, list 52, 2000, no.60.*

However, the majority of Celtic warriors did not wear any body armour at all, but fought in "heroic nudity". This custom was still current on the Continent in Caesar's day, but whether or not it was for religious reasons is unknown. (James 77).

It is on coins of Tasciovanus that the mintmarks VER-, VERL- or VERO- first appear, indicating Verlamio or Verolamio. There is a similar mark on a bronze coin, which shows on the obverse two bearded male heads, one overlapping the other; on the reverse is a ram and a sun symbol.[21.]

*Fig.77. Catuvellauni, Tasciovanus (first coinage). Gold quarter stater, 12mm, 25-20 BC.
VA 1690.
Crossed wreaths. VERO in angles.
Celticised horse left, TAS below horse, bucranium above horse.
Sternberg AG, Zürich XII, 1982, 7.*

Fig.78. Catuvellauni, Tasciovanus (first coinage). Bronze unit, 16mm, 25-20 BC.
VA 1705.
Celticised heads right, hair made up of short curls.
Celticised ram left, TASC above ram, "wild flowers" before and below ram.
Leu AG, Zurich 86, 2003, 45.

Fig.79. Catuvellauni, Andoco. Gold stater, 17mm, 10 BC-AD 10.
VA 1860 var; dJ 54.
Crossed wreaths; hidden faces.
Romanised horse, bucranium and ring-pellet motif above horse AND O below and in front of horse.
Ex Chris Rudd. (not in list)

In about 10 BC, late in Tasciovanus' reign, there appears a series of coins with the legends AND(OCO), DIAS-, SEGO- and RVES- , sometimes in conjunction with the king's own name. What we unfortunately do not know is whether these abbreviations represent personal names. If they do, perhaps they were the names of sub-rulers within this king's domain, or else officials charged with particular responsibilities.[22.]

Addedomaros, ruling over present day Essex, was succeeded by Dubnovellaunus (not to be confused with the similarly named ruler who was striking coins in Kent at that time).[23.] His coins are distinguished by a palm branch beneath the horse, the symbol of the Roman goddess of victory, Victoria. The carefully-designed symmetry of the obverse, unlike most Celtic coins, leaves plenty of space, so that the wreath design can be fully appreciated.

Fig.80. Catuvellauni, Sego. Gold stater, 17mm, 10 BC-AD 10.
VA 1845; dJ 54.
Reverse Celtic warrior on horse right, brandishing carnyx.
SEGO in front of horse.
Kruta page 79.

Fig.81. Dubnovellaunus in Essex. 30-25 BC.
VA 1655; dJ 56.
Crescents and wreath.
DVBNOVILLA. Horse left, branch below and legend and ring pellet motif above horse.
Leu AG Zürich 59, 1994, 5.

Fig.82. Dubnovellaunus in Kent. Silver unit, 12mm, 30-23 BC.
VA 165.
Beardless Celticised head left, DVBNO in front of head.
Pegasus right, box with cross-hatching below Pegasus.
Leu AG, Zürich 86, 2003, 4.
Chris Rudd list 64, 2002, 21.

The Sons Of Commius

It was probably the Essex Dubnovellaunus whom Augustus refers to along with the Atrebatic Tincomaros[24.] in his **Res Gestae** ("My Achievements") (**Res Gestae** 32, 1). Tincomaros, the son of Commius, had been driven out after a dynastic squabble with his brother Epillus, while Dubnovellaunus had been a victim of the expansionist policies of the Catuvellauni, who were extending their lands at the expense of the Trinovantes (Brodersen 49).

The early coins of Tincomaros, stamped with TINCOM- or TINC- COMM- F (or in the case of quarter staters, simply a single T), have all the appearance of an early coinage, since at the end of the 1st century BC a complete change of style occurred.

Fig.83. Atrebates, Tincomarus (Tincommius) (first coinage). Gold stater, 16mm, 30-25 BC.
VA 363; dJ 38.
Celticised head of Apollo right.
Celticised horse with triple tail right, six spoked wheel below horse. TIN above horse.
CNG 57, 2001,1656.

Fig.84. Atrebates, Tincomarus (first coinage).
Gold quarter stater, 10mm, 30-25 BC.
VA 366.
Wreath, pellet in centre.
Horse right, T above horse.
Tkalek AG Zürich, 2002, 2.

Fig.85. Atrebates, Tincomarus (third coinage). Gold stater, 18mm, 20-10 BC.
VA 385.
COM F in tablet.
Warrior holds spear, TIN below horse.
Chris Rudd, list 54, 2000, 18.

Fig.86. Atrebates, Tincomarus (first coinage).
Gold quarter stater, 9mm, 30-25 BC.
VA 365.
TIN COM in two lines in tablet.
Celticised horse left.
Leu AG Zürich 86, 2003, 12.
Chris Rudd, list 38, 1998, 14.

*Fig.87. Atrebates, Tincomarus (first coinage). Silver unit,
11mm, 30-25 BC.
VA 370.
Celticised head facing.
TIN above bull, C below bull.
Schweizerische Kreditanstalt 1987, 5.*

*Fig.88. Atrebates, Tincomarus (third coinage). Silver unit,
12mm, 20-10 BC.
VA 397.
Romanised head right; head laureate and beardless.
Eagle stands with spread wings. Both obverse and reverse
adapted from denarii of Augustus.
CNG 57, 2001, 1662.*

From now on Roman *denarii* from the late Republican period to the time of Augustus began to serve as models, with types such as Victory, Apollo, and Cupids riding upon dolphins. Also popular were Pegasus, butting bulls, facing eagles or Medusa heads. It is quite likely that Roman die cutters were working for Tincomaros, which of course suggests a close relationship with Rome.[25.]

*Fig.89. Atrebates, Tincomarus Medusa type. Gold quarter
stater, 10mm, 25-20 BC.
VA 378.
TINC in tablet, C above and A below tablet.
Medusa head facing.
CA may indicate Calleva mint.
CNG 57, 2001, 1659.*

*Fig.90. Atrebates, Tincomarus (first coinage). Silver unit,
12mm, 30-25 BC.
VA 371.
Star or "wind flower".
Boy riding dolphin right, TINC below dolphin. Reverse
adapted from a denarius of L. Lucretius Trio or Mn.
Cordius Rufus.
CNG 57, 2001, 1665.*

*Prototype: Denarius of Mn. Cordius Rufus, 18mm, Seaby I,
Cordia 3.*

Fig.91. Atrebates, Epillus (Kentish type). Gold quarter
stater, 9mm, 10 BC-AD 10.
VA 435.
EPPIL COM F in two lines.
Pegasus right.
CNG 57, 2001,1669.

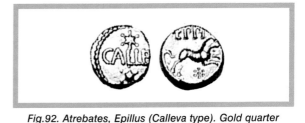

Fig.92. Atrebates, Epillus (Calleva type). Gold quarter
stater, 9mm, 10 BC-AD 10.
VA 407.
CALLE(VA). Six-pointed star above and below inscription.
Horse right. EPPI above horse.
Triton I New York, 1997, 2207.

While the coins of Tincomaros are concentrated
in the southern parts of the Atrebatic kingdom, those
of his brother Epillus crop up mainly in the region of
Calleva (Silchester). Like Tincomaros, Epillus calls
himself REX on his coins, and son of Commius. The
abbreviations CALL- and CALLEV- for Calleva are a
reliable indicator of the mint.

Fig.93. Atrebates, Epillus. Gold quarter stater,
9mm, 10 BC-AD 10.
VA 409.
COMM F EPPILLV around crescent.
Celticised horse right.
Tkalek AG, Zürich, 2002, 3.

Fig.94. Atrebates, Epillus. Silver unit, 13mm, 10 BC-AD 10.
VA 416.
Celticised head right, beard made up of pellets.
Boar right, EPPI above, F CO in two lines below boar.
Chris Rudd, list 54, 2000, 23.

Pedigrees

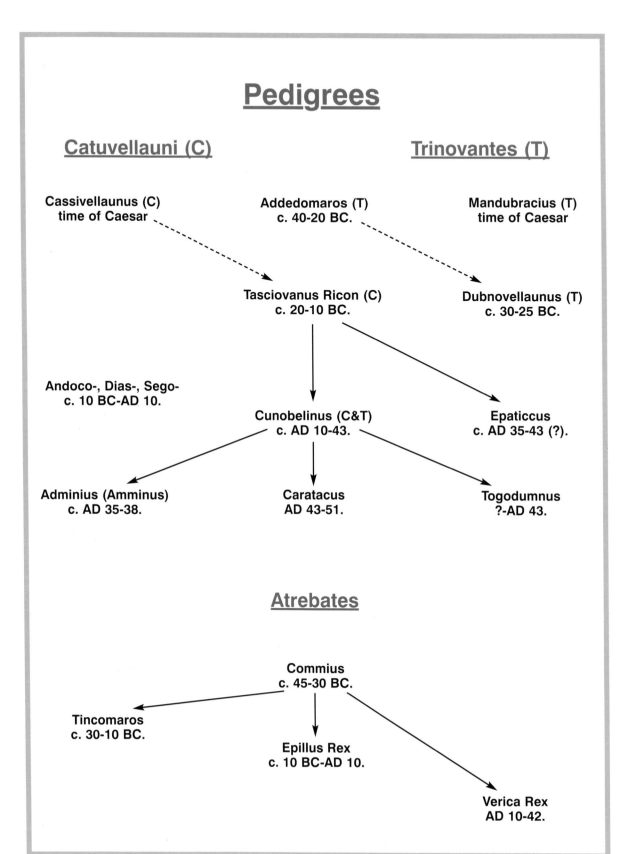

Catuvellauni (C)

Cassivellaunus (C)
time of Caesar

Trinovantes (T)

Addedomaros (T)
c. 40-20 BC.

Mandubracius (T)
time of Caesar

Tasciovanus Ricon (C)
c. 20-10 BC.

Dubnovellaunus (T)
c. 30-25 BC.

Andoco-, Dias-, Sego-
c. 10 BC-AD 10.

Cunobelinus (C&T)
c. AD 10-43.

Epaticcus
c. AD 35-43 (?).

Adminius (Amminus)
c. AD 35-38.

Caratacus
AD 43-51.

Togodumnus
?-AD 43.

Atrebates

Commius
c. 45-30 BC.

Tincomaros
c. 30-10 BC.

Epillus Rex
c. 10 BC-AD 10.

Verica Rex
AD 10-42.

Chapter 6

The British Policy Of Augustus & His Successors

In 34 BC, and again in 27 or 26 BC, it appears that Augustus had considered the invasion of Britain, but on each occasion he decided he had other priorities. After long years of wars and civil conflicts, his dream was of a single realm that stretched from Cadiz on the Atlantic to the mouths of the River Elbe, also encompassing, eventually, the lands of the German tribes. In approximately 25 BC he closed the gates of the Temple of Janus, and proclaimed the Pax Augusta.

Later, however, due to the failure of his German policy, he quietly dropped his plans for an invasion of Britain, and called this "wise government". Even the pleas for help, mentioned earlier, from the British chieftains Tincomaros and Dubnovellaunus, which could have been justification enough for a Roman invasion, failed to move Augustus to change his policy (**Res Gestae** 3, 1). This new policy trend caused even the achievements of Julius Caesar to be looked at again, and re-evaluated. His two British expeditions came to be seen no longer as a continuation of, or a finishing touch to his conquest of Gaul, but more as an unnecessary adventure into another world - perilous, and at the same time completely profitless (**Velleius Paterculus** 2, 46, 1., Brodersen 52).

Under Tiberius (AD 14-37), whose policy was to remain within existing borders, there was peace. Britain was quietly forgotten, it seems. It is not mentioned at all by the sources during Tiberius' reign.

At about this time, Cunobelin (circa AD 10-43) and his successors of the Catuvellauni tribe, were becoming a major factor in the politics of Celtic Britain. Cunobelin worked systematically and determinedly at increasing his territory at the expense of his neighbours, until at length he began to threaten the interests of Rome. For a time, the only obstacle to his ambitions was Verica or Bericos (circa AD 10-42), king of the Atrebates and son or grandson of Commius. In the intrigues and power play for dominance over the fertile south east of Britain, Cunobelin set up his brother Epaticcus and his sons Adminius (or Amminus), Togodumnus and Caratacus as sub-rulers, and did not hesitate to play one off against the other, when it suited him.[26]

The accession to the throne of Gaius (AD 37-41), the son of Germanicus and Agrippina Senior, was welcomed with enthusiasm by the Roman army and people alike, after the death of the dour Tiberius, whose hatred of the human race had made him totally unpredictable. The nickname of Caligula, "Little Boots", had begun with a soldiers' joke, because he had spent his early years in military camps, dressed in the miniature uniform of a legionary (Suetonius, **Caligula** 9, 1).[27] It was perhaps the combination of a serious illness, coupled with panic attacks, acute insomnia and the loss of his sister Drusilla that led first to mental disorder, and finally to a complete breakdown in the young emperor's character.

From being the darling of the people, he changed by degrees into "the very model of an insane tyrant, whom, in the evil of his name, only Nero rivals". (Scarre 41). In order to win prestige, Caligula prepared plans in AD 39 for nothing less than the complete conquest of both Germany and Britain. One of the reasons for the expedition against Britain was once again the flight of a local prince Adminius (or Amminius as he is called on his coins), who had been driven out by his father Cunobelin, or his brothers (Suetonius, **Caligula** 44).

After a few insignificant skirmishes on the Rhine, Caligula led his army to the English Channel, but the expected invasion of Britain did not follow. A mutiny amongst the soldiers, who feared to cross the sea, and perhaps also a belated realisation of the risks of the undertaking, turned Gaius from his plan. Instead, as though a great victory had been won, he ordered *"the entire army, drawn up in battle order, to march to the water's edge, followed by the artillery and other heavy equipment. No one had the faintest idea what was in his mind. Then, suddenly, he ordered that the men should pick up seashells, and fill their helmets and pouches. This was to be, according to him, the tribute from Ocean, which was due to the Capitol and Palace"* (Suetonius, **Caligula** 46). The only remaining trace of this expedition today is a huge tower at Boulogne, an imitation of the lighthouse on the island of Pharos at Alexandria. The murder of Caligula in AD 41 ended Rome's interest in Britain for the time being.

At about the same time, certainly no later than AD 43, Cunobelin, the Cymbeline of Shakespeare's play, died. He is seen today, rightly, as **the** ruler of Celtic Britain. His influence extended unopposed over the lands of the Catuvellauni and the Trinovantes. Through his brother Epaticcus he dominated the Atrebates, and members of his clan ruled as far away as Kent. Through its control of the cross-Channel trade, his kingdom had become an economic power to be reckoned with. Great quantities of luxury goods and consumables were imported from Gaul and the entire Mediterranean with wine, in particular, being a popular item in high demand. Exports included wool, pottery, cereals and various raw materials.

Chapter 7

The Coinages Of Cunobelin

The boom in trade was the principal reason why, under Cunobelin, a cash economy became - even for minor transactions between individuals - so widespread. The proof of this is the huge quantity of base metal money that now appears consisting of masses of low value coinage in bronze and other alloys. But it was not only bronze issues that proliferated; the issues of gold coins, too, became a flood. It has been estimated that during a period of about 30 years, more than a million gold staters were struck.

Under Verica the Atrebates during the same period produced only about a third of this quantity (VA 393). The building housing Cunobelin's mint, identifying itself by the marks CAMVL-, CAMV-, or CAM-, has been discovered and excavated in Colchester.[28.] Its early gold coins, such as the "Biga" type, follow closely the style of Tasciovanus. It may well be that the reverse type of a triumphal biga celebrates his coming to power (de Jersey 36).

The characteristic type on the coinage of Cunobelin is the ear of corn. This design can be interpreted two ways. One explanation is that corn was the most important local crop, being both the staple foodstuff and also an important ingredient of the local beer - a striking contrast, therefore, with the vine leaf of his rival, Verica. Alternatively, it might simply have been copied from a coin of Metapontum in Lucania.

Fig.95. Catuvellauni and Trinovantes, Cunobelin (Biga type). Gold quarter stater, 12mm, AD 10-20. VA 1913; dJ 57. Inscribed wreath and tablet: CAMVLO (AMV in ligature). Two Celticised horses left, leaf above horses. CVNO below horses. Triton V Zürich 2002, 2426.

Fig.96. Cunobelin. Gold stater, (classic type). 18mm, AD 20-43. VA 2027; dJ 58. Corn ear, CA MV to left and right of corn ear. Romanised horse right, branch above horse. CVN below horse. CNG 63, 2003, 1918.

Fig.97. Cunobelin. Gold quarter stater, (plastic type).
11mm, AD 20-43.
VA 2017.
Corn ear. [C]AM in ligature to left and CV to right of
corn ear.
Celticised horse right, branch above horse [CVN] below.
R. Pudill.

Fig.98. Cunobelin. Gold stater, (reverse). 17mm, AD 20-43.
VA 2029; dJ 58 var.
Corn ear, CA MV to left and right of corn ear.
Chris Rudd, list 54, 2000, no.75.

Fig.98a. Atrebates, Verica (Third coinage). Gold stater,
17mm, AD 25-35.
VA 520; dJ 42.
Vine leaf. VI RI to left and right of leaf.
Chris Rudd, list 49, 2000, no.20.

Fig.99. Lucania, Metapontum. Silver stater, 21mm, c.480-400 BC.
Head of Demeter right.
METAΠO. Corn ear.
Leu AG Zürich 86, 2003, 237.

The silver and bronze coinages of Cunobelin generally follow Roman patterns, such as, for example, the seated Victory, the Sphinx, or the helmeted head, copied from the head of Roma on Republican coins.

Fig.100. Cunobelin. Silver unit, 14 mm, AD 20-43.
VA 2045 var.
Romanised head left, CAM in front of face, VL behind head.
Seated victory right. CVNO below chair.
Reverse adapted from a Roman denarius of
M. Porcius Cato Uticensis.
Chris Rudd list 54, 2000, 77

Fig.101. Cunobelin. Silver unit, 12mm, AD 20-43.
VA 2057.
Winged bust right, CVNO in front of face.
Sphinx left, TASCIO in front of sphinx. Reverse adapted
from a Roman denarius of T. Carisius or Augustus.
R. Pudill.

Fig.102. Prototype. Augustus. Aureus, 20mm, 27 BC-AD 14.
Head of Augustus right.
Sphinx right.
Künker 83, 2003, 666.

Fig.103. Cunobelin. Bronze unit, 15mm, AD 20-43.
VA 2091.
Romanised head (Roma) right. CVNOBELINVS around head.
Sow standing on exergual line. TASCIIOVANI F around sow.
Triton I Zürich 1997, 2219.

There is a bronze coin of Cunobelin on which both sides imitate an original of Augustus. The obverse bears the head of the first emperor, while on the reverse is a butting bull, symbol of the power and dominance of Rome, especially now in Gaul.

Fig.104. Cunobelin. Bronze unit, 15mm, AD 20-43.
VA 2095.
Romanised head (Augustus) right.
CVNOBELINVS REX around head.
Bull butting right. TASC F below exergual line.
Chris Rudd, list 63, 2002, no.75.

Fig.105. Prototype. Augustus denarius, 19mm,
27 BC-AD 14.
Seaby I 137.
Head of Augustus right.
Bull butting right.
R. Pudill.

Cunobelin's descent from Tasciovanus is underlined by a bronze coin, bearing the design of Pegasus and Victory above a bull, with the inscription TASCI-. Pegasus again is a type found on the *denarii* of Augustus.

Fig.106. Cunobelin. Bronze unit, 15mm, AD 20-43.
VA 2099.
Pegasus right, CVNO below Pegasus.
Victory sacrificing a bull right. Tasci below bull.
Chris Rudd, list 73, 2004, no.72.

Fig.107. Prototype. Augustus denarius, 19mm,
27 BC-AD 14.
Seaby I 491.
Head of Augustus right.
P PETRON TVRPILIAN III VIR.
Leu AG, Zürich 33, 1983, 10.

Another bronze of Cunobelin from Camulo-dunum bears the striking and powerful portrait of a young man. On the reverse a female hound is shown trampling a serpent, while apparently holding at bay a rearing, double-headed reptile. Among the Celts, and the Romans too, the dog was seen as a faithful friend to man, but at the same time as a symbol of the Underworld, or the world to come and as man's companion on the journey there. The serpent in ancient times could have positive or negative significance for man, but mostly mythology portrays the sinister, even devilish aspects of this darkness-loving creature. It was brought forth from the earth, and is therefore often used to personify that which is earthly or evil, in contrast to that which is heavenly or good.

Fig.108. Cunobelin. Bronze unit, 14mm, AD 20-43.
VA 2131.
Head left CAMVL in front of face.
Female hound left, serpent in front and below dog.
CVNO below dog.
Chris Rudd list 54, 2000, 79.

Other coins of Cunobelin are clearly derived from earlier originals, such as bronzes with a reclining lion, or a sphinx, or Perseus holding the severed head of Medusa. There is also a coin bearing the head of Zeus-Ammon, showing great resemblance to a *denarius* of Marc Antony (Seaby 1a; BMC 3; Syd. 1280). Possibly this representation of a ram-horned god was intended to be the Celtic war god Camulos-Mars (the word "camulos" or "camalos" means ram in Celtic). (Birkhan 462 ff).

Fig.109. Cunobelin. Bronze unit, 17mm, AD 20-43.
VA 2107.
Head of Jupiter Ammon right. CVNO in front of face.
Lion right, tree behind and CAM in tablet below lion.
Triton V Zürich 2002, 2427.

Fig.110. Prototype. Mark Antony. Denarius,
19mm, 31-30 BC.
Seaby I Mark Antony 1a.
Jupiter Ammon right.
ANTONIO AVG SCARPVS IMP. Victory.
Ex H.A. Seaby, Roman Silver Coins 1,121, 1a.

Fig.111. Cunobelin. Bronze unit, 15mm, AD 20-43.
VA 2109.
Sphinx right, CVNO on exergual line.
Perseus holds Medusa head in right hand, staff in left.
CA beside Perseus.
Chris Rudd, list 74, 2004, no.69.

Although Roman types seem to have been preferred as originals, still earlier coins were also copied, including some quite rare Greek issues. For example, the standing warrior on a bronze of Cunobelin derives from a coin of Aitna in Sicily. On well-preserved examples, the details of his clothes and weapons can be clearly seen, as with the horseman on the obverse (de Jersey 37).[29.]

Fig.112. Cunobelin. Bronze unit, 16mm, AD 20-43.
VA 2093.
*Celtic warrior on horse right, CVNOB around scene.
Cunobelin Warrior type. Standing warrior with helmet, spear and shield left.
Chris Rudd list 53, 2000, 87.*

Fig.113. Prototype. Aitna Sicily. Bronze unit,
19mm, c.210 BC.
*D.R. Sear I, 1018. Bust of Apollo right.
Standing warrior holding spear and shield.
Ex D.R. Sear, Greek Coins I, 1018.*

At the same time there were some quite separate styles developing, for example this symmetrically arranged floral design.

Fig.114. Cunobelin. Bronze unit, 13mm, AD 20-43.
VA 2049 var.
*Floral pattern. CA M left and right beside pattern.
Sphinx (?) right. CVNO below the exergual line.
Chris Rudd list 54, 2000, 78.*

One silver coin of Camulodunum - apparently unpublished and supposedly found on the Hungarian/Serbian border - bears on both sides an ear of corn and the letters "CAM". The only possible interpretation of this find is that the coin found its way there along a trade route from Britain.

Fig.115. Cunobelin (?). Silver unit, 13mm, c.20-40 BC.
*Corn ear. CA M left and right beside corn ear.
Corn ear. [CA] M (?) left and right beside corn ear.
R. Pudill.*

Chapter 8

Epaticcus

Epaticcus of the Catuvellauni (circa AD 35-42) ruled, by consent of Cunobelin, over the northerly parts of the Atrebatan lands; that is to say, the areas surrounding Calleva. Nothing could really make any clearer the bonds between them than the striking of a gold stater bearing the ear of corn, the classic symbol of Cunobelin, his "brother". The only difference is that the lettering CAMV is replaced by TASCI F, standing for Son of Tasciovanus. The reverse shows a mounted warrior, with shield and spear, galloping right, and the legend EPATI.

Fig.116. Epaticcus. Gold stater, 18mm, AD 25-35.
VA 575 (Atrebates!).
TAS to left CI F to right of ear.
Celtic warrior on horse right. EPATI below horse.
Ex Chris Rudd, (not in list).

Another coin, this time a silver unit, bears a seated Victory and a boar, once again very similar to the parallel issue of Cunobelin.

Fig.117. Epaticcus. Silver unit, 12mm, AD 25-35.
VA 581.
Seated Victory right TASCIOV around Victory.
Boar right, tree behind. EPAT on exergual line.
Triton II, Zürich 1998, 1221.

This realistically drawn boar, however, appearing on a small silver coin, with wide open jaws and exaggerated tusks, seems to have no direct origins.

Fig.118. Epaticcus. Silver unit, 8mm, AD 25-35.
VA 585.
EPATI between pellet-in-ring motifs.
Boar's head right. TA below boar's head.
Chris Rudd, list 53, 2000, 41.

This next coin, with its bearded male head and leaping lion, is almost classical in its appearance. Above the beast is a cross, or cloverleaf shape, reminiscent of the Egyptian Ankh, the symbol of life. Its legends, TASCIO and EPATI, like most of his other coinages, do not expressly describe Epaticcus as being the son of Cunobelin. Thus it may well be that Epaticcus was his grandson, not his son. F(ilius) may well imply successor here, and not son.

Fig.119. Epaticcus. Silver unit, 13mm, AD 25-35.
VA 582.
Bust left. TASC in front of face, IO behind head.
Lion right. Flower (?) above lion. EPATI beneath.
CNG 57, 2001, 1707.

The next coin is unquestionably copied from a classical original. Although unusual on a Celtic coin, Hercules wearing the lion-skin appears on this silver coin of Epaticcus. On the reverse appears a facing eagle, its wings outspread and its head turned to the left. In its claws a serpent writhes, symbolising all that is earthly. The eagle was the bird of sun and sky, and in harmony with this there appears above the bird a cross, the symbol of the sun. We may interpret this scene as portraying the victory of the divine over the earthbound, or alternatively over the powers of darkness.

Fig.120. Epaticcus. Silver unit, 11mm, AD 25-35.
VA 580.
Bust right. EPATI in front of face.
Eagle facing, holding serpent in claws.
Chris Rudd, list 60, 2001, no.32.

Chapter 9

The Coinage
Of Verica

It is possible that Verica (circa AD 10-42) who, like Tincomaros and Epillus, called himself COM F, son of Commius, was in fact not the son but the grandson of the dynasty's founder. The dates of the two princes also suggest that in this case *filius* should be understood as meaning successor rather than son.

At the beginning of his reign, Verica appears to have exercised control over the entire territory of the Atrebates, but in about AD 30 to 35, he was compelled to yield a considerable part of the north of his kingdom to Epaticcus. This seriously lessened the area he ruled, reducing it to just the southern parts of his original territory. Because of this, he was obliged in AD 42 to beg Claudius for help against the repeated incursions of the Catuvellauni, and their allies the Trinovantes.

In about AD 30, Verica begins to call himself REX on his coins, the Latin word for king, rather than RICON, the Celtic equivalent, perhaps to underline his new status as a client king of Rome. His name appears on his coins in various forms (eg as VIR, VIRI, and VERI), as well as in its complete form of VERICA. On some issues, his name disappears entirely, and only the enigmatic legend COM F, combined with the styles and find spots, allows us to make the correct attributions to this ruler.

This quarter stater belongs to the early years of Verica's reign. On the obverse it bears the legends COM FILI above and below a thunderbolt. On the reverse is a realistically depicted horse, beneath which is a symbolic sun; in the top right field are the letters VIR.

Fig.121. Atrebates, Verica. (first coinage). Gold quarter stater, 10mm, AD 10-20.
VA 468.
Inscription and scroll pattern. COM above and FILI below two curved lines.
Horse right. VIR above horse.
Leu AG Zürich 86, 2003, 18.

This silver fraction with the inscription VIRIC on the obverse and a boar on the reverse also belongs to the early issues of Verica from his mint of Calleva. The silver units bearing the legend COM F in a right angle with a front facing eagle, and those bearing a galloping horse on the reverse, are of similar date.

Fig.122. Verica. Silver, 8mm, AD 10-20.
VA 423, 510-1.
VIRIC in plain field.
Boar right. C above.
Leu AG Zürich 86, 2003, 19.

Fig.123. Verica. Silver unit, 13mm, AD 10-20.
VA 471.
COM F in tablet.
Eagle facing with wings spread.
Chris Rudd, list 78, 2004, no.24.

Fig.124 Verica, Atrebates. Silver unit, 12mm,
AD 10-42.
VA 530.
Chris Rudd, list 48, 1999, no.38.

Fig.125. Verica. Gold quarter stater,
10mm, AD 10-20.
VA 466.
COM F in tablet
Horse right. VI above horse.
Triton IV, Zürich 2000, 935.

After about AD 20 to 25, a change comes over the style of Verica's coinage, linked with the beginning of the Catuvellaunian expansion. On their obverse the coins now proclaim Verica's descent from Commius (COM F, VERIC COM F or else VERICA COMMI F). Beside a horse or lion, symbolising kingly power, the title REX underlines his claim to kingship (which, however, was more of a wish than a political reality).

Fig.126. Verica (second coinage). Gold stater, 17mm,
AD 20-25.
VA 500.
COM F in incuse tablet.
Celtic warrior on horse right. VIR above, REX below horse.
Chris Rudd list 54, 2000, 24.

Fig.127. Verica (second coinage). Gold quarter stater,
10mm, AD 20-25.
VA 501.
VERIC COM F in two lines.
Horse right. REX below horse.
Chris Rudd list 54, 2000, 27.

Fig.128. Verica (second coinage). Silver unit, 13mm,
AD 20-25.
VA 505.
VERICA REX around large ring.
Lion right, REX beneath.
CNG 57, 2001, 1685.

This silver coin, with its types of a butting bull, and a left standing figure bearing a branch, with the legends VERICA REX and COMMI F once again harks back to Roman originals.

Fig.129. Verica (second coinage). Silver unit, 13mm,
AD 20-25.
Bull right. VERICA inverted above bull,
REX below exergual line.
Figure holding branch in right hand. COMI F around figure
Chris Rudd list 54, 2000, 29.

To his third and final coin issue belongs the well-known gold stater, struck at a mint somewhere in the south and bearing the vine leaf on one side, and a mounted warrior on the other (regarded usually as a contrast to Cunobelin's corn ear type). The possibility should not be ignored, however, that it is not a vine leaf represented here. The design could perhaps be an imitation of a silver coin of Selinus in Sicily, which bears the leaf of the selinon or wild celery plant, chosen by that city as its numismatic symbol solely as a play on the name. Shown on coins, its leaves are almost indistinguishable from those of the vine.

Fig.130. Verica (third coinage). Gold stater, 18mm,
AD 25-35.
VA 520.
Vine leaf. VI to left and RI to right of leaf.
Celtic warrior on horseback right. CO F in field.
Leu AG Zürich 59, 1994, 3.

Fig.131. Selinus, Sicily. Silver didrachm, 24mm, c.520-490 BC.
Sear 1, 730. BMC 2.5.
Selinon leaf.
Incuse square.
Leu AG Zürich 59, 1994, 63.

Two silver coins of Verica clearly derive from the "tribute penny" - the commonest *denarius* of Tiberius - with the emperor's portrait on the obverse and Livia as Pax on the reverse.

Fig.132. Prototype. Tiberius. Silver denarius, AD 14-37.
Seaby 2, 16. BMC 34.
Head of Tiberius right.
Livia as Pax seated right.
Tkalek AG Zürich, 2000, 233.

The two sides of a Celtic coin were sometimes copied from different originals, as for example the crossed cornucopias and caduceus on a *quinarius* of Marc Antony, symbolising the restoration of trade and prosperity.[30.] The types of Roman coins were, in this case, re-struck in completely different combinations.

Fig.133. Verica (Third coinage), AD 25-35. Silver unit, 12mm.
VA 533.
Bust of "Tiberius" right, VIRI behind bust, CA in front of face.
Male figure standing left, holding lituus in right hand.
CNG 57, 2001, 1688.

Fig.134. Verica (third coinage), AD 25-35. Silver unit, 12mm.
VA 531.
Crosses cornucopiae. COMMI F
Seated figure right (Livia as Pax). VERI CA.
CNG 57, 2001, 1687.

Chapter 10

The Invasion Of Britain

Even though Cunobelin had managed to avoid provocations toward Rome, and thus any irreparable breach with the superpower, Togodumnus and Caratacus, his sons and successors, were far from possessing the diplomatic skills of their father. They extended their territories without thought of the consequences. The lands of the Cantii passed into their power, and through force of arms they gained control over at least part of the tribal lands of the Dobunni. They then pressed so hard on the Atrebates that Verica (Berikos) was forced to capitulate to them.

Shortly after the accession of Claudius in AD 41, this son of Commius came to Rome to beg the emperor for protection from the aggressors, and to ask for military intervention. The prince chose his words well, and succeeded in re-awakening imperial interest in the far-off island. He spoke of the riches to be found there - gold, silver and other metals - and even pearls, the gifts of Ocean (Agricola 12, 6).

Claudius did not really need these inducements, because he had his own weighty reasons for wanting a successful military campaign. However, this plea for help from the Atrebates, requesting Rome to honour her undertaking to her British client kingdom, was a useful *casus belli*. Claudius, who had unjustly acquired the reputation of being a foolish and vacillating ruler, desperately needed military glory in order to secure the loyalty of his generals and soldiers. Nothing less than his political survival was at stake, or perhaps even his life.

To command the expedition, Claudius selected the experienced and well respected senator Aulus Plautius. In the year AD 43 Plautius marched to the Channel coast, with four legions and approximately the same number of auxiliary troops (a total of some 40,000 men in all), with the intention of making the crossing.[31.] However, just as had happened three years earlier under Caligula, the soldiers refused to leave the *oikumene*, the boundaries of the known world (Dio 60, 19, 1-2). With the assistance of the influential imperial chancellor Narcissus, Plautius tried to persuade the soldiers, but without success. Yet suddenly, and for no apparent reason, Dio tells us they changed their minds. With a shout of "*Io Saturnalia*", they declared themselves ready to risk the adventure, to chance the terrifying Ocean crossing, and to take on the Britons in their "far-off" island, lying "beyond all civilisation".[32.]

The crossing, from Gesoriacum (Boulogne-sur-Mer), was made in three separate divisions, and was completed without incident. The main force disembarked in the natural harbour of Rutupiae (Richborough), in the present day county of Kent, while a second squadron reached Chichester.

Togodumnus and Caratacus had joined forces in Kent, but faced now with superior Roman numbers, they withdrew inland. In the vicinity of a river (probably the Medway), they made a stand. In the ensuing battle, Togodumnus was killed, and Caratacus, heavily defeated, fled for his life.

Further fighting took place near the lower reaches of the Thames, possibly at the site of present day London. Dio relates that not only the "barbarians" but the Romans too suffered serious losses in the impenetrable swamps which lined the far bank. This persuaded Plautius not to attempt any further advance, but instead to consolidate what he had already won (Dio 60, 20, 5-21, 1). In these two battles, the future emperor Flavius Vespasianus, his brother Sabinus, and Gaius Hosidius Geta particularly distinguished themselves, the latter receiving the highest possible award, the *ornamenta triumphalia*, for his bravery in action.[33.]

After these initial successes, and the subsequent lull that followed, Plautius requested the emperor to come in person, since "without his intervention, no decisive battle would be possible". As an experienced diplomat, the legate wished to create the impression that Claudius alone was in a position to bring the campaign to a favourable conclusion. Meanwhile, Plautius prepared the ground well for the decisive battle. After taking over the chief command of the army, Claudius crossed the river and inflicted on the barbarians, who had assembled in great force to meet him, a shattering defeat, seizing Camulodunum, the capital of Cunobelin (Dio 60, 21, 4). He next disarmed the defeated tribes, and placed them under the authority of Plautius, together with the instruction that he should "get on with conquering the rest" (Dio 60, 21, 4).[34.]

Claudius had spent all of 16 days in Britain, but it was enough for him to be awarded a full triumph. The Senate voted him the conqueror's title of Britannicus, and erected in his honour a triumphal arch, which with the shortened inscription DE BRITANN appears on his coinage.[35.]

Fig.135. Claudius (AD 41-54). Denarius 19mm.
Seaby 2, 18; BMC 35.
Head of Claudius right.
DE BRITANN on triumphal arch, surmounted by equestrian figure between two trophies.
Leu AG Zürich 57, 1993, 242.

Claudius was not slow to honour those Senators who had taken part in the campaign. They received triumphal insignia, and Plautius himself was awarded an *ovatio*, a minor triumph.[36.]

Once the fighting was over and the fertile lowlands secured, everything east of a line running from Exeter to Lincoln, later known as the Fosse Way, was organised into the Province of Britannia. Aulus Plautius was installed as its first Imperial governor, with the title of *legatus Augusti pro praetore*.

In AD 49, in the area of Camulodunum, the old capital of the Trinovantes, the first colony of veterans on British soil was established, *Colonia Claudia Victricensis*, so named in honour of the Legion XX Valeria Victrix. The city was the residence of the Imperial governor, the seat of the cult of emperor worship, and also a legionary base. The governor had many responsibilities: military affairs, and the supporting infrastructure, such as the developing network of roads; handing down legal judgments, where Roman citizens were concerned; and diplomatic relations with the *civitates*, the tribes and cities of the native peoples. Beside the *legatus Augusti pro praetore*, a procurator was appointed who was responsible for running the finances of the province. This official, originally stationed in Camulodunum, probably moved his residence quite early on to the newly founded city of Londinium (London), far better sited from a practical point of view.

In order to safeguard the province's borders, and also to establish some sort of control over neighbouring tribes, treaties were signed with the rulers of the Brigantes of the Pennines, and the Iceni whose lands lay in the north eastern part of the Roman province. Henceforth, their kings were to be regarded by the Romans as friends and allies. In order to safeguard their rights and independence, these two client states made common interest with Rome - both sides pledged themselves to give the other military assistance as it became necessary.

One ally in particular is brought especially to our attention by Tacitus - Togidumnus. In his **Agricola**, Tacitus relates that *"certain domains were presented to King Cogidumnus, who maintained his unswerving loyalty right down to our own times - an example of the long established Roman custom of employing even kings to make others slaves"*. (**Agricola** 14, 1). But who was this man, and what was it that caused Claudius to regard him as the successor of Verica, and in recognition of his loyalty to present him with the overlordship of the Regni? And how comes it that an inscribed monument found in Noviomagus Regnensium (Chichester) hails him as *rex magnus Brit(annorum)*?[37.] We just do not know, and the most we can say with certainty is that this king appears to have played an important part in the first phase of the conquest of Britain. He might have been one of those kings who travelled to see Augustus in Rome but whom, unfortunately, that emperor fails to name. Perhaps Togidumnus returned to Britain in the train of Claudius, and from then on devoted his life to serving the interests of the Empire.

Chapter 11

Resistance & Rebellion Against The Roman Occupation

Aulus Plautius' successor as Imperial governor of Britain, P. Ostorius Scapula (AD 47-51/2), taking up his office late in AD 47, found the province far from peaceful. First there was a rebellion among the Iceni, who had resented the confiscation of their weapons. War could not be avoided. The Iceni fought with remarkable heroism, probably under the command of their new king, Prasutagus, whose reign began in about AD 47 or 48 and lasted until about AD 59 or 60. This revolt, however, was soon put down by superior Roman power.

Almost simultaneously there was a threatened rising among the Brigantes but this, however, was quelled by the personal intervention of the governor.

Worse yet was the situation in the west, present day Wales, where Caratacus, the son of Cunobelin - although beaten in early engagements by the Roman invasion force - had still not been decisively defeated. Assisted by various Welsh tribes, principally the Silures and the Ordovici, and spreading a message of "Freedom or Slavery",[38.] he

had succeeded in uniting opposition to the Roman presence in Britain.

Scapula moved against him with the XXth Legion, recently transferred from Camulodunum to Glevum (Gloucester), and beat him a second time in the year AD 50. Caratacus' wife and daughter were captured, while he fled to Cartimandua, queen of the Brigantes. She, however, mindful of her obligations as an ally of Rome, handed him over. Claudius, in an act of magnanimity and "as a lasting monument of his clemency" spared the life of this, the last ruler of the house of Cunobelin, as well as his wife and brothers (Ann 12, 37).

The historical Caratacus, who briefly succeeded Epaticcus as ruler over the northern parts of Atrebatic territory, issued two silver coins. His short reign saw a silver unit with the head of Herakles and the eagle. It differed from the issue of his predecessor Epaticcus only in the legend CARA, and abbreviated form of his name. On the other known type of Caratacus, a fraction, the letters C A R A are

Fig.136. Caratacus, Atrebates. Silver unit, 12mm, AD 43-51.
VA 593; dJ 44.
Bust right. CARA in front of face.
Eagle with spread wings facing, holding serpent in claws.
Schweizerische Kreditanstalt 7, 1987, 28.

Fig.137. Caratacus, Atrebates. Silver unit, 8mm, AD 43-51.
VA 595; dJ 44.
CARA around pellet-in-ring motif.
Pegasus right.
Chris Rudd list 54, 2000, 32.

arranged symmetrically around a symbolic sun, and the reverse bears a Pegasus.

The resistance of the Silures to the invaders continued unabated, however, even after the defeat of Caratacus, causing the Romans several severe setbacks. Scapula had great difficulty coping with their form of guerrilla warfare, and finally died "of grief over his fruitless toils", according to Tacitus (Ann. 12, 39).

His successor, A. Didius Gallus (AD 52-57), at first took the offensive, but as time went on he became increasingly defensive minded, and finally contented himself with merely holding the ground he had won (Agr. 14). However, it was the Brigantes who presented the real problem. The client-queen Cartimandua, having fallen out with her husband Venutius, an implacable enemy of Rome, used her wiles and cunning to bring his brother and other relatives into her power. Then, because these men had "allowed themselves to fall into the hands of a wench", her enemies were outraged, and determined to move against her; the queen therefore found herself in an extremely perilous position.

Rome felt itself compelled to abandon its policy of non-interference in dynastic squabbles. Cartimandua was indeed rescued by Roman troops, but Venutius seized power, which was to lead to a *de facto* end to the client kingdom in AD 69. (Ann.12, 40; Hist. 3, 45).

Didius was succeeded by Q. Veranius, of a family close to the Julio-Claudian dynasty. His grandfather had been guardian of Drusus, and his father a friend of Germanicus. After the assassination of Caligula, he had led a deputation to Claudius, and it was he who had persuaded him to accept the purple. He was therefore regarded as the emperor's right hand man.

Veranius opened a new offensive in North Wales, but died before completing his first year in office.[39] He was succeeded as governor by C. Suetonius Paulinus (AD 58-61), a man carefully selected for his experience in mountain warfare. Paulinus took up the campaign against the tribes of Wales, determined to force a decisive battle. Final victory over the stubborn island was long overdue for, since the command of Claudius in AD 43 to conquer "the rest" of Britain, 15 years had now gone by. Claudius was now dead and Nero ruled in Rome.

After two successful thrusts into South and North Wales, Paulinus made preparations for the invasion of the island of Mona (Anglesey). Mona was not taken, but only because of the great revolt of Boudica, which had thrown the entire province into uproar, and whose suppression was to demand from the Romans their last reserves of effort and strength.

Mona was the centre of the entire island's Druidic activity and the spiritual centre of resistance to Rome. It was a refuge for every rebel and runagate - or, seen through other eyes, patriots and freedom fighters. Even Tacitus, usually so neutral and compassionate in his reporting, follows Roman propaganda by describing their "horrid religious rites", in order to justify the campaign against the Druids, and the destruction of their holy groves. He tells us that *"their religious ceremonies demanded that the blood of captives should be shed upon the altars of sacrifice, and that the will of the gods should be learned from the bowels of the victims"* (Ann.32).[40]

We are relatively well informed about the rebellion of Boudica, thanks to the narratives of Tacitus (Ann 14, 29-39; Agr, 15-16) and Cassius Dio (Dio 62, 1-12). But several important questions remain unanswered, such as the site of the final battle, and the exact duration of the revolt. Dio, writing some 140 to 150 years after the event, has left us with a description of Boudica's character and appearance. According to him, Boudica (or Buduica)[41] was, in his words, *"cleverer than women usually are"*, and *"of an imposing, even terrifying aspect"*. Her voice was harsh and powerful, and her red-blond hair fell to her hips. Around her neck she wore the symbol of her rank - a heavy gold torque. Beneath a woollen mantel, pinned by a brooch, her robe was brightly patterned in the Celtic fashion. So arrayed, a spear in her hand, and perhaps standing in a war chariot, the widow of the Roman's client-king delivered a burning speech to the Iceni and their allies. Her intention was to fill them with courage for the coming battle, whose outcome would determine freedom or slavery for the Celtic race.

Following Tacitus' example, Dio puts words into Boudica's mouth, which reveal his compassion for her oppressed people, and his admiration for their heroic resistance. Rhetorically, the royal widow asks:

"What manner of humiliation and torment have we not had to endure, since these people [the Romans] first appeared in Britain?....How much better would it have been to go down in defeat and death, rather than to live with their yoke upon our necks!....How can it be, that although none of us possesses great wealth, yet we are fleeced and robbed like the victims of footpads?" (Dio 62, 1-3). In an impassioned speech, Boudica swears to her countrymen, her friends and her relatives that she will never allow her children to grow up in slavery, not knowing what freedom is. Boudica, whose name is synonymous with Victoria, is convinced she will be victorious, and emphasises the superiority of her native warriors, who know the ground, and are used to bearing hunger, thirst, heat and cold. The Romans, in her eyes, are pampered mollycoddles, who *"loaf in shade and comfort, their thoughts only on their soft bread, their wine and their olive oil"*. (Dio 62, 5, 5.).

Her speech closes with the words *"Let us show them how far they presume, rabbits and foxes that they are, when they would try to rule over hounds and wolves"*. (Dio 62, 5, 6). She finished, and the masses before her roared their applause. Boudica then raises her hands to heaven, and says: *" I thank thee, O Andraste, and call to thee as woman to woman....As queen of such [valiant and battle-hardened men], I beg and beseech thee that thou wilt grant us victory, salvation and freedom....* (Dio 62, 6).[42.]

This fictitious speech of Boudica's on the morning of the decisive battle explains the reasons behind the revolt, which almost led to the loss of the entire province. Tribal lands had been seized and a *colonia* for veterans had been built at Camulodunum. The Celtic ruling classes, already having regular tribute exacted from them, had now been forced to borrow heavily in order to pay for the provincial administration, the cult of the emperor, and the building and maintenance of the temple dedicated to Claudius at Colchester. Now these loans were being called in, plus interest, which was totally beyond the means of the Trinovantes, on whose shoulders most of the burden would fall.

Neither did they intend to stand for it. They joined themselves with the rebellion of the Iceni, who had compelling reasons of their own for launching an armed uprising against the Romans.

Prasutagus, the husband of Boudica, had been installed as client king by the Romans - probably in AD 47 at the time of the first Icenian revolt. In his will, he divided his lands equally, leaving half to the emperor, Nero, and the remainder to his wife and daughters. He hoped in this way to avoid the total absorption of his lands into the Roman province. However, after the king's death some time in AD 59 or 60, the Romans regarded his will as being in no way binding upon them - rather, they saw it as a *carte blanche*, allowing them to help themselves to whatever they wanted.

The arrogant attitude of the Roman officials, especially of the procurator, Decianus Catus, enraged the Iceni, and the situation became daily more explosive. Finally, when Boudica was punished for her complaints against Roman officers by being publicly whipped, and her daughters raped, this huge revolt, which had been brewing for some time now, was triggered, and the royal widow was to be its figurehead.

Circumstances were in favour of immediate attack by the rebel army. The XIVth Legion and most of the XXth were tied up in Wales and Mona (Anglesey) with Suetonius Paulinus, and the provincial capital was poorly defended, unwalled and held only by a small garrison. Consequently Boudica with her Iceni and their Trinovantian allies marched first on Camulodunum. A call for help from the veterans there to Catus in London was at first not taken seriously; and then a mere 200 men were sent.

The insurgents took Camulodunum with little difficulty. The city was completely destroyed, and the temple of Claudius, where a group of retired soldiers and their families had taken refuge, was set on fire and burnt to the ground. A relief force of 2,000 legionaries and cavalry from the IXth Legion - based in the north under Q. Petilius Cerialis - made for Colchester, but marched straight into an ambush, and were driven off with appalling losses. Only Cerialis and his mounted men got away.

Poenius Postumus, the *praefectus castrorum* temporarily in command of the Legion II Augusta stationed in the west, refused orders either to march on Camulodunum or to join Paulinus (either through practical difficulties, or else for fear that his legion too would be wiped out). When matters finally turned out in Rome's favour, Postumus took his own life, either from shame or else to avoid punishment. Even the procurator Decianus Catus abandoned his post, and fled to Gaul (Dio 62, 8,2).

It was only through the sheer determination of Paulinus that the province was not entirely lost. While Boudica and her army, estimated at up to 200,000 strong, were marching on St. Albans and London, Suetonius and his cavalry were hastening to meet her by forced marches. His infantry, the greater part of his army, were following, but without them he was hopelessly outnumbered by the enemy horde. If it came to a battle, he would have had no chance at all, and so he had no option other than to retreat before them. He had to watch helplessly, as the two principal cities of the province were taken and burnt, their garrisons wiped out, and thousands of civilians slaughtered. The situation had become so desperate that Nero considered abandoning the province, and it was only piety towards his adoptive father Claudius that persuaded him otherwise (Suetonius, **Nero** 18).

It was probably at Viroconium (Wroxeter) that Paulinus and his mounted force were reunited with his army, consisting of the XIVth Legion, part of the XXth, the remainder of the IXth, and attached auxiliary units - a total of some 10-15,000 men. They advanced down the Roman road known today as Watling Street, and headed for Verulamium.

Somewhere near Lichfield they met the British horde, so sure of victory that *"they had brought their womenfolk with them, and had placed them on wagons around the edge of the battlefield"* (Ann 14, 34, 2). Making skilful use of the ground, the experienced general and tactician Paulinus won the day. The Iceni and their allies were slaughtered. Some 80,000 Britons and 400 Romans are said to have fallen on that bloody day, when even the lives of women and draught animals were not spared (Ann 14, 36, 2-37, 3).

Altogether, Boudica's revolt had cost the lives of some 150,000 people,[43] not counting the civilian casualties - a terrible blow for the infant province. The entire work of 17 years was as good as lost. After this disaster, Boudica took her own life, *"by poison"* according to Tacitus (Ann. 14, 37, 3). Dio's account is that she *"fell ill and died"* (Dio 62, 12, 6). He adds the following note: *"The Britons mourned her loss bitterly, and built for her a magnificent tomb"* (Brodersen 109 ff).

Some time in the winter of AD 60-61 a new procurator, Gaius Julius Alpinus Classicianus, arrived in Britain. His report to the emperor, that there was never going to be peace in the province as long as Paulinus was in charge, was probably the reason behind the appointment of a new governor, P. Petronius Turpilianus (AD 61-63). Turpilianus succeeded in re-establishing Roman authority over the southern part of the island without being unduly repressive.

Chapter 12

The Final Celtic Coins Of Britain

There is now little question that the coin ascribed by Van Arsdell to Boudica is really much earlier, having been struck about 70 years before her death.[44.]

Fig.138. Early Icenian type. Silver unit, 13mm.
So-called Boudica.
VA 794; dJ 83.
Chris Rudd, list 64, 2002, no.38.

There is one extremely rare and historically important coin which has been dated to the reign of Prasutagus, the Roman client king, and husband of Boudica. This coin bears on the obverse a Romanised head reminiscent of Nero, and on the reverse a slightly stylised horse, with a crescent above and a "sun-anemone" below. The unusual obverse and reverse legends SVB RI PRASTO ESICO FECIT (under King Prasto, made by Esico) give us the names both of the king as issuer, and of his mint master.[45.]

Fig.139. Prasutagus, Iceni. Silver unit, 13mm, c.AD 50-60.
VA 780; dJ 88.
Romanised head left. SVB RII PRASTO inscribed around
head. Ring and pellet motif in front of head.
Celticised horse right. ESICO FECIT inscription around horse.
CNG 57, 2001, 1761.

The Roman style of the coin, together with the Latin inscriptions and the naming of the mint official, combine to indicate pro-Roman leanings in the issuing authority, and also date the coin to after the Roman conquest, probably somewhere between AD 45 and 60. With the death of Prasutagus and the suppression of Boudica's revolt, Celtic independence comes to an end, and with it Celtic coinage.

Recently, questions have been raised about the correct meanings of incomplete obverse legends on all Celtic coins known to date, and further doubt has been cast by Parsons upon their attribution. The name of the ruler upon a coin found in Norfolk[46.] with a fuller inscription reads (according to Parsons and Williams) ESVPRASTO or ESVPRASCO (Esuprastus), which would seem to agree with the six gold staters of the Corieltauvi belonging to a hoard from Silsden. If this turns out to be correct, then *"we can no longer say with certainty that Prasutagus was the name of an Icenian king, nor the husband of Boudica"*. (Parsons).[47.] In his **Annals**, while outlining the origins of the revolt, Tacitus refers to the Icenian king Prasutagus specifically by name, and therefore in our view this conclusion of Parsons cannot be correct (**Annals** 14, 32, 1). It is, however, not impossible that the coin he attributes to the husband of Boudica belongs in fact to some other ruler, as yet unknown, of the AD 50s.

Chapter 13

The "Conquest Of The Rest"

The 10 years that followed the revolt of the Icenian queen and her allies were devoted to consolidating the Roman province. Not until after the suicide of Nero in AD 68 was there renewed Roman expansion in Britain.

Cartimandua, the client queen of the Brigantes, lost her throne to her husband Venutius, and an attempt by the governor M. Vettius Bolanus (AD 69-71) to reinstate her proved abortive. His successor, Q. Petilius Cerialis, opened a new offensive to the north, in the course of which he penetrated into the northwest of the island, as far as Luguvalium (Carlisle) on the course of the future Hadrian's Wall.

In this campaign against the Brigantes, the future governor Agricola played a leading part, commanding the XXth Legion. Under Sex. Julius Frontinus (AD 73-77) a fresh offensive in Wales was opened, and after a victory over the Silures most of mainland Wales came under Roman control. By this time all the client kingdoms had been absorbed, apart from that of Togidumnus, but how long this exception lasted is unknown.

Cn. Julius Agricola (AD 77-84), later to be the father-in-law of the historian Tacitus, made it his goal to complete the subjugation of the entire island, and this was the prime policy of his term in office. And so, after a campaign against the Ordovici and the final capture of the Druids' stronghold of Mona (Anglesey), he turned his attention to the tribes of southern Scotland. By AD 79 he had passed the isthmus between the Clyde and the Forth (**Agricola** 23),[48.] and by 80 or 81 he had reached the north-west coast of Scotland.

Two years later, his fleet reached Trucculensis (? or T(h)ulensis) portus, possibly the harbour of the fabled land of Ultima Thule, the Shetlands. (**Agricola** 38, 4).[49.]

As well as being a good soldier and general, Agricola was also an administrator of exceptional ability. The network of Roman roads, essential for speedy troop movements, was extended. Agriculture was improved, as were food storage arrangements, in order to guarantee the supply of provisions to the military anywhere in the province.

Agricola actively promoted the Roman way of life, and encouraged the provincial towns in the building of temples, forums and better dwelling houses. In this way, he achieved his ends through *"rivalry for honour rather than by compulsion and oppression"*. People now began to enjoy the baths and festivals, and those who *"previously had loathed the Latin language, now eagerly studied to speak it well"*. And, he adds, *"the toga was now everywhere to be seen"* (**Agricola** 21).

In his sixth year of office, Agricola pressed yet farther north, supported by his fleet, and built a fortress at Inchtuthil on the Tay. In the following year, AD 83, he brought the Caledonians under Calgacus and their allies to battle at Mons Graupius, which is perhaps identifiable with Mount Bennachie at Inverurie, some 25 miles north west of Aberdeen, if not still further north.[50.]

Tacitus tells us that, following ancient custom, before the battle began the two leaders addressed their men, to raise their spirits and give them courage. Calgacus attacked the Roman's insatiable greed and thirst for glory, and their wish to force even this, the last corner of a free land, under their yoke. *"Now the farthermost bounds of Britain lie open. To robbery, butchery and rapine they give the lying name of "government". They make a desert, and they call it peace"*[51.]

(**Agricola** 30). The Romans won a bloody victory at Mons Graupius, and now all Britain lay at their feet (**Agricola** 35, 2-38; **Hist.** 1, 2, 1).

But just a few years later the Romans withdrew, and Inchtuthil was abandoned in AD 86 or 87. The reasons behind this were probably not, as Tacitus supposes, the jealousy of the emperor Domitian (AD 81-96) towards the successful and popular Agricola (**Agricola** 39-41), but rather the realisation that the conquest of the impenetrable Scottish highlands had brought Rome little benefit, and that the Empire had much more serious problems on the Danube.

Hadrian (AD 117-138) a ruler interested primarily in peace and security, inspected the province in AD 122. One of the reasons behind his visit was an intended reorganisation of the province's garrison, following a revolt among the northern tribe of the Brigantes in AD 117, which had not been fully suppressed until the following year by the new governor, Q. Pompeius Falco (AD 118-122).

Fig.140. Hadrian (AD 117-138). Sestertius, 32mm.
BMC 1313.
Bust of Hadrian, laureate, right.
Hadrian in military dress on horse prancing left, raising right hand.
R. Pudill.

North of a line of forts on a road known as the Stanegate, which runs between Solway and Tyne, Hadrian built the Wall which still bears his name. (HA Hadr. 11, 2.). The construction of this 73 mile long stonework, numerous mile castles and turrets, a system of ditches on either side, and eventually with 16 forts along its line, served as a useful programme for keeping the troops busy and maintaining discipline. At the same time it allowed a far greater control over the movements of travellers and goods in both directions.[52.]

Fig.141. Hadrian (AD 117-138). Sestertius, 31mm.
BMC 1484.
Bust of Hadrian, laureate, right.
Hadrian advancing right, holding baton in left hand, followed by a centurion and three soldiers.
The soldiers carry vexilla. In exergue DISCIPLINA AVG.
R. Pudill.

Fig.142. Hadrian (AD 117-138). Sestertius, 31mm.
BMC 1673.
Head of Hadrian right
Hadrian standing right, raising right hand, haranguing three soldiers holding legionary
eagle, vexillum and shield. In ex.: EXERC BRITANNICVS.
Lanz, München 94, 1999, 504.

Under Antoninus Pius (AD 138-161) the frontier again moved north, but Marcus Aurelius (AD 161-180) returned it to Hadrian's Wall. With short interruptions, the Wall remained the northern boundary of the province (later the diocese) of Britain, until shortly before the final abandonment of the island by the Roman authorities in the year AD 410.

Fig.143. Hadrian (AD 117-138). As, 24-27mm.
BMC 1175.
Bust of Hadrian right.
Britannia seating facing, foot on rock, resting head on right hand,
holding sceptre in left; to right large shield.
R. Pudill.

The period following the Roman withdrawal, called the Dark Ages, was not as gloomy as the name suggests. It is not generally realised how thin in many places had been the veneer of Roman civilisation that overlaid Celtic culture. Originating in Irish monasteries, there began a rich Celtic literature, which set down in Celtic languages a host of traditional myths and legends, previously passed down only in word or song. Hence a wealth of ancient texts survived, which otherwise would have been lost forever.

Ireland's monks created, via the delicate tapestries of their handwriting, an impressive, almost *"intoxicating artistic language, with which they wove together the ideals of Christianity with the ancient images of their Celtic past"* (Siemons 50).[53.]

Almost half a millennium after the end of Celtic civilisation, their culture underwent a renaissance in Ireland. Scottish missionaries from Ireland brought it, via Britain, back to the Continent, where, mingling with other traditions, it became a leading element in the formation of Western culture.

Notes

Time Line

BC	ROME	CELTS
800	753 Traditional date of the founding of Rome.	800 Proto Celts
700		
600		Hallstatt Period.
500	510 The rule of kings is replaced by an oligarchy in the form of a Republic.	
400	400 Italy invaded by Celtic tribes. 387 Rome is besieged and sacked by Brennus.	450 Beginning of the La Tène period. Celtic migration reaches Britain. The first Celtic coins to be struck in Gaul, copied from the silver pieces of Massilia. The import of La Tène goods to Britain begins.
300	280 Roman coinage now becomes universally accepted. 264 First Punic War begins. 225 Wars against the Celts.	Area of Celtic settlement reach its greatest extent. Gold staters of Philip of Macedon copied by the Celtic tribes of Gaul.
200		The first Gallic coins, of the Ambiani tribe, are imported into Britain. 120 The first wave of Belgic migration reaches Britain. The first indigenous Celtic coins are struck by the Cantii, followed somewhat later by the Trinovantes & Catuvellauni.
100		
80		80 Second wave of Belgic migration into Britain. 75 First coins of the British Atrebates.
60	The first Triumvirate: Pompey, Caesar, and Crassus. Caesar becomes Consul.	
58	Beginning of the Gallic War.	
57	Caesar installs Commius as king of the Gallic Atrebates.	
56	Mandubracius, prince of the Trinovantes, begs Caesar for help against Catuvellaunian aggression.	Commius reconnoitres Britain, and prepares for Caesar's invasion.
55	Caesar's first expedition to Britain.	Caesar achieves only minimal success against his principal opponents in Britain, the Catuvellauni.

BC/AD	ROME	CELTS
54	Caesar's second expedition to Britain, five legions strong, meets with only mixed success.	The British Celts unite behind Cassivellaunus in the struggle against Caesar. Cassivellaunus submits to Caesar. "The entry of Britain into history".
53	Britain is now seen as falling within Rome's sphere of influence. Revolts against Caesar in Gaul, led by Vercingetorix.	Commius joins the Gallic Celts in their struggle against Caesar.
50	The Gallic War ends with the fall of Alesia and the capture of Vercingetorix.	The Atrebate Commius escapes to Britain, and there founds a dynasty, which endures until the time of Claudius.
45 44 27-14 27 25	Caesar becomes Dictator for Life. Caesar is murdered on the Ides of March. Octavian/Augustus Augustus contemplates an invasion of Britain, but later finds other priorities. *Pax Augusta*.	Dubnovellaunus and Tincomaros seek sanctuary from Augustus (*Res Gestae*).
20 JC		Tasciovanus (circa 20-10 BC) king (Ricon) of the Catuvellauni.
10		Cunobelinus (circa 10-43 AD) of the Catuvellauni becomes an important factor in the power play in Britain.
14-37	Tiberius "*Sub Tiberio quies*"	The Trinovantes are forcibly united with the Catuvellauni. Camulodunum (Colchester) becomes the capital of the new kingdom. The brother of Cunobelinus, Epaticcus, and his sons Adminius, Togodumnus and Caratacus receive the status of client kings. Cunobelinus issues coins of Roman style.
37-41	Gaius (Caligula)	
39	Gaius plans an invasion of Britain that, however, comes to nothing.	Adminius attempts to persuade Gaius to make war on his father Cunobelinus.
41-54	Claudius	Death of Cunobelinus (42/43)
43	Claudius entrusts Aulus Plautius with the conquest of Britain. Plautius defeats the sons of Cunobelinus, thereby bringing the South-East of Britain under Roman control. Claudius spends just 16 days in Britain. Camulodunum captured. Claudius instructs Plautius to "conquer the rest of the island". Britain is established as a Roman province. Aulus Plautius (43-47) installed as its first governor. His successor	Verica of the Atrebates, a son or grandson of Commius, begs Claudius for assistance against the Catuvellauni. Plautius lands with four legions at Rutupiae (Richborough). Battle at the River Medway. Death of Togodumnus. Flight of Caratacus. Plautius' seat of government becomes Camulodunum. The limits of the Province are undefined, but run approximately from present day Exeter to Lincoln (The Fosse Way).

AD	ROME	CELTS
47	P. Ostorius Scapula (47-51/52) arrives, to find conditions unsettled.	Scapula puts down a rebellion of the Iceni under their king Prasutagus. Camulodunum is granted the status of *colonia*. The Welsh tribes of the Silures and Ordovici rebel against Rome, under the leadership of Caratacus. Caratacus seeks refuge with Cartimandua, queen of the Brigantes, who hands him over to the Romans.
52	A. Didius Gallus (52-57)	Renewal of the offensive in Wales. Trouble from the Brigantes.
54-68	Nero	
58	C. Suetonius Paullinus (58-61)	Attempted conquest of the Druids' island of Mona (Anglesey).
59		Death of Prasutagus. The final Celtic coinage: SVB RI PRASTO ESICO FECIT.
60	The arrogance of the Roman officials leads to the revolt of the Iceni and Trinovantes under the leadership of Boudica, widow of Prasutagus, leading almost to the total loss of the Province.	Revolt of Boudica. Camulodunum, Londinium and Verulamium (St. Albans) are totally destroyed. Heavy losses on both sides.
	Paullinus defeats Boudica in a pitched battle.	Boudica dies, or takes her own life.
69	Galba/Otho/Vitellius (Year of the three emperors).	
69-79	Vespasian	
69	M. Vettius Bolanus (69-71)	Rome's ally, Queen Cartimandua, is overthrown by the Brigantes.
71	Q. Petillius Cerialis (71-73)	A new offensive in the North brings the frontier to Luguvalium (Carlisle).
73	Sex. Iulius Frontinus (73-77)	Victory over the Silures.
77	Cn. Iulius Agricola (77-84) undertakes the "conquest of the rest".	Conquest of Mona (Anglesey) and parts of Caledonia (Scotland).
81-96	Domitian	
83		Decisive battle against the Caledonians and their allies at Mons Graupius. However, parts of Wales and Scotland still remain unconquered.
96-98	Nerva	
98-117	Trajan	
117-138	Hadrian	
118	Q. Pompeius Falco (118-122)	Revolt among the Brigantes.
122	Hadrian visits Britain.	Construction of Hadrian's Wall between Solway Firth and the mouth of the Tyne. The Wall is completed by 136.

Notes

1. For more on the Celtic pantheon, religion and Druidic cult, see Maier; Herm pp 187-201; Noelle 145-219; Matschoss 40-43; Moreau 99-108, and the so-called Gallic Excursion in Caesar's **Gallic Wars**, 6.11 et seq.

2. Similar to the development of the portrayal of Celtic gods is the appearance on Alexandrian coins of the Roman Imperial period of a god in the form of an animal, for example Horus represented by a falcon. Sometimes, parallel to this, and following the Greek idea, the god appears in human form, accompanied by the relevant animal or symbol as an attribute. Interestingly, the double-axe symbol is also found on the Egyptian local coinage of the Nome of Oxyrhynchites.

3. Further reading on Celtic money systems and coin production from the 3rd to the mid 1st century BC can be found in: Moreau 92-98; Kruta 106-127 and 140 onward; Demandt 34 et seq; Duval, particularly 263 et seq (prototypes) and map 454 (directions of the spread of prototypes).

4. For metal bars used as currency, see Thomas Lautz, in "Das Fenster" at the Kreissparkasse Bank, Cologne. Theme 163 of April 2003; and VA 1 et seq. Also see Rudd 'Earth money' (Chris Rudd list 74, 2004, 4-7).

5. The name of Albion applied to Britain appears first during the 4th century BC in Pytheas of Massilia, and implies "Highland-island", probably because of the chalk cliffs of Dover. Alb in Celtic means "heights", and inn "land" or "island". It is quite possible that the merchants questioned by Caesar deliberately misled him with their exaggerated descriptions of the riches to be found in Britain.

6. VA 201-1 to 202-1 attributes the Westerham type solely to the Atrebates (75-60 BC), while Rudd also gives them to the Trinovantes of Essex and Suffolk (Chris Rudd, Aylsham, Norfolk, List 54, 2000, no.71).

7. The term "potins" means cast coins of various alloys of copper, tin, lead and silver. They were cast in strips in clay moulds, and then broken off from the central bar formed by the pouring channel. On many potins a trace of the casting strip is still visible. In Britain, finds of potins are concentrated around Kent and the lower reaches of the Thames.

8. Denarii of Caesar RRC 452/2; 452/4; and 468/1.

9. The ram, the ram's horn, and indeed the ram-headed serpent were all sacred to Teutates. Misleadingly, rams' horns correctly portrayed on coins as thickened at the roots are often described in numismatic literature as bulls' horns. The "multi-face" phenomenon appears on many Celtic coins, for example, the stater of Tasciovanus, king of the Catuvellauni.

10. Rudd suggests a medlar, or more likely a crab-apple branch, due to the similarity between the Celtic word ceri (crab apple) and Cori(nium), the capital of the Dobunni; or, alternatively, the name of the tribal chief Corio (Rudd list 53, 2000, 63). Rudd also proposes that the tree-like emblem may be derived from the budding branch of a coppiced ash tree (Chris Rudd list 72, 2000, 7-15).

11. The practice of completely filling up the surfaces of coins with designs, leaving no space whatever unfilled, is known, very appropriately, as *horror vacui*.

12. VA 184; Rudd 53, 49 and 54, 39.

13. VA 80-1; Rudd, list 41; Rudd, list 53, 50.

14. VA 790-1 to 794-1; Rudd list 53, 53 (he calls this type "Norfolk God"); and de Jersey 49. See also Rudd 'The Boudica myth' (Chris Rudd list 58, 2001, 5-11).

15. VA 321; de Jersey 33 et seq.

16. The title of a Celtic king was rigs, Hellenised as "ricon". The Indo-Germanic root means "to direct". From this root comes the Latin "rex", and the Indian "rajah". Among Celtic rulers, the syllable rigs or rix often appears as a suffix to their personal names, for example, Vercingetorix, Ambiorix, etc. (Demandt 76).

17. The beards of the three faced god from Soissons consist of wheat ears. Beneath, not visible in the illustration, are carved the creatures sacred to Mercury, the ram and the cock, which indicates that this is in fact the Celtic Teutates, who was identified with Mercury.

18. This richly decorated and partly gilded silver cult vessel, dating from the 1st century BC, was

found in a peat bog near Gundestrup in Jutland. It appears to originate from the eastern fringes of the Celtic cultural areas, but how it got as far as Jutland, to be thrown into the bog as a sacrifice, is unknown. The designs on both the outside panels and the inner side of the bowl show male and female deities, partly surrounded by exotic beasts, symbols and signs. This cult object is of immense interest, both iconographic and mythological, and also gives valuable information about the weapons and equipment of the Celtic warrior (Duval 183 et seq.).

19. Diodorus 5, 30: *"They are armed with shields the height of a man, painted in a most particular way. On some of these, elaborate brazen animal figures, of the most skilful workmanship, have been fixed....The brazen helmets, with which they protect themselves, have towering crests, which cause them to appear extraordinarily tall. These are either in the form of horns, welded on to the helmet, or else the faces of birds or four-footed animals fixed to the helmet itself. Their trumpets have a peculiarly barbaric tone to them producing harsh notes, which accord well with the tumult of war. Some wear iron suits of mail; others fight naked."* Diodorus Siculus goes on to tell us that the Gauls rubbed lime into their hair, and then combed it back from the top and sides, which lent them the appearance of so many Satyrs or Pans, increasing their apparent size and fierceness. (See also James 77).

20. Detail from Picasso's "Paseo de cuadrillas", the entry of the toreadors into the arena, Cannes, Spring of 1957. Page 3 of the "Tauromaquia". Collection Sprengel I/693.

21. Chris Rudd gives the Celtic name for St. Albans as Verlamio. The correct spelling of the abbreviated name on coins would then be VERL-, and not VERV-for the Latin Verulamium. This, however, does not explain the equally common form VERO-

22. Plutarch mentions a hierarchic system, with delegation of authority and responsibility, and while speaking of the Celts, he uses the term Tetrarchs to mean rulers over one quarter, or even smaller portions, of a kingdom (Demandt 76).

23. Several writers have put forward the idea that Dubnovellaunus of Essex and the similarly named ruler of Kent are one and the same person (Birley, people, 23); Rainer Kretz 'From Kentish lad to Essex man: The Enigma of Dubnovellaunos', (Chris Rudd list 31, 1998, 1-6).

24. Tincomaros, or Tincommius, which names mean "the great fish", are in fact alternative spellings for one and the same ruler; it is now agreed that Tincomaros is the correct spelling.

25. The *denarius* of Mn. Cordius Rufus, struck in 46 BC (Seaby RSC Vol I, Cordia 3) was used as a prototype for the coin with the six-pointed star and boy on the dolphin.

26. In the power play for overlordship, Cunobelin set up members of his clan as puppet sub-kings in the regions bordering his own tribal lands, such as his son Amminus in Kent, and his brother Eppaticus in the northern part of Atrebatan territory. In some numismatic books and papers (eg VA and Rudd), the ancestry or tribe of a ruler is not a decisive factor, but rather the town or the territory covered by his coinage, which can lead to serious confusions. As an example of this, Epatticus, the son of Tasciovanus is attributed to the Atrebates, while his father Tasciovanus is given to the Catuvellauni; and Caratacus, son of the Catuvellaunian Cunobelin, is assigned to the Atrebates. Much clearer is the system of Philip de Jersey, who correctly outlines descent and tribal origin, and classifies the coins geographically, as, for example, North Thames, South Thames, and so on.

27. According to Suetonius, Caligula 44, Adminius was driven out by his father, the British king Cynobellinus (Shakespeare's Cymbeline). Whether Adminius is the same person as the Amminius known from coins found in Kent is unclear.

28. The name Cunobelin derives from *cuno* - hound, and Belinus/Belenos. The Celtic Belenos was identified by the Romans with Apollo. The name Cunobelinus thus means "hound of Belenos". The hound, in the form of a psychopompos, was the attendant animal of Apollo. Cunobelin's mint building at Colchester/Camulodunum has been discovered and excavated.

29. Aitna in Sicily, AE trias of circa 210 BC. Obverse: Radiate bust of Apollo right. Reverse: Warrior standing, with spear and shield. Sear, **Greek Coins & Their Values** 1978, Vol.1, 1018; BMC 2.1.

30. Mark Antony (circa 40 BC). M ANT IMP III VIR R P C, BMC 115; Syd. 1189; Seaby 66. The choice of design because of the similarity of the VIR in the legend of the Antony coin to the abbreviated form of the name Verica - VIR cannot be coincidental.

31. The expedition to Britain was composed of the Legions IX Hispana, under the command of Aulus Plautius; II Augusta from Strasbourg, commanded by the future emperor Vespasian; XIV Gemina from Mainz; and XX Valeria Victrix from Neuss.

32. Dio gives a detailed report on the invasion of Britain (Dio 60, 19-21). During the Saturnalia,

slaves and their masters used to exchange places. Dio speaks of *beluosus Oceanus* (meaning frightful, full of monsters) and *ultimi Britanni* (the farthermost dwellers of the known world).

33. The emperor alone might celebrate a triumph, the highest honour for military conquest.

34. It took another 40 years, and the battle of Mons Graupius in AD 83 or 84, for the exceptionally able general and governor Agricola to succeed in fulfilling the command of Claudius to "conquer the rest", and even then success lasted for only a short time.

35. In this abbreviated inscription, DE might stand for devicta (conquered), or else DE BRITANN may mean de Britannis (Victory) over the Britons. The complete (and partly restored) inscription reads: "To Tiberius Claudius, Son of Drusus, Caesar Augustus Germanicus, Pontifex Maximus, in the year of his eleventh tribunicia potestas, five times Consul, twenty-two times Imperator, Censor, Father of the Fatherland (this has been dedicated) by the Senate and People of Rome, for having conquered eleven kings of the Britons without any loss whatever, and for having first brought the barbarian nations beyond the Ocean under the power of the Roman people" (ILS 216).

36. For further information on triumphs and victory celebrations in ancient Rome, see K. Künzl: **Der römische Triumph**.

37. RIB 91. The formal title of a governor implies senatorial rank. Brodersen and Barrett interpret the damaged part of the inscription as reading "rex magnus Britannorum" or "Regis magni Britanniae", which has the meaning of "supreme king", perhaps a title originating in Celtic tradition. (Brodersen 77 et seq; Barrett 124 et seq.) For the full story of Togidubnus see Martin Henig, The heirs of King Verica, Tempus 2002.

38. Ann. 12, 34,2. A fictitious speech of Caratacus before the decisive battle.

39. A.R. Birley, Das römische Britannien, Heinrich-Heine-Universität Düsseldorf, Summer Term 2002.

40. Caesar confirms the fact that human sacrifice was a normal part of Celtic religion.

41. The Celtic name Boudica, or Buduica (Old Welsh buddug) signifies Victoria.

42. This is the only place where the war goddess Andraste is mentioned by name. It is probably her portrait which appears on a silver coin of the Iceni (VA 80; BMC 3524-26; Ev. 115; M 438).

43. Dio says 230,000 men (Dio 62, 8,2), Brodersen has 120,000 (Brodersen 104).

44. Iceni, "early Face/Horse type; see also chapters Iceni/Eceni; VA 213; de Jersey 49 et seq.

45. H. Mossop's reading of the legend. Van Arsdell reads: SVB RII PRASTO ESICO FECIT. VA 213 et seq: de Jersey 51 et seq.

46. CNG 57, 1761.

47. The hoard is dated to the mid 1st century, the time of Cunobelin. Cecilia Parsons in her Internet article mentions Jonathan Williams, whose research work should be conclusive on this subject.

48. According to A.R. Birley, Agricola began his term of office in Britain in AD 77. (Birley, Fasti, 73-81). The isthmus between the Firth of Clyde and the Firth of Forth, that is to say approximately between present day Glasgow and Edinburgh, was under Antoninus Pius, briefly the northern frontier of the province. A few years later it was withdrawn to the Solway-Tyne line - Hadrian's Wall.

49. That the Roman fleet reached the Shetland Isles seems certain. The Trucculensis harbour mentioned by Tacitus might well be the same as Thule (A.R. Birley, Address on Roman Britain, Heinrich-Heine-University Düsseldorf, Summer Term 2002).

50. The remarks quoted by Tacitus in the speech of Calgacus: "Now the farthermost bounds of Britain lie open" and "Here humanity ends; beyond, there is nothing more than the waves of the sea" give grounds to set the battlefield further north. See Jones, 76 et seq.

51. These words from the fictitious speech of Calgacus, before the battle of Mons Graupius "*Ubi solitudinem faciunt, pacem appellant*" have become a well known saying.

52. This mighty system of fortifications, with its walls and ditches, running from present day Carlisle to Newcastle and beyond, was not only a means of "separating the Romans from the barbarians" (HA Hadr. 11,2). Just as important, it was a 10 year building project and work program for the troops. Hadrian was aware that in time of peace nothing was more dangerous for the stability of the Empire than idleness among the soldiers. The Wall was not built completely in stone - in the west, where stone was scarce, turf was used.

53. Ch. Hainzinger; Herkunft und Erbe der Kelten. In: Geschichte 4, 2003; Fries-Knoblach 54.

The Sources

Gallic Wars -   Caesar: **Commentaries on the Gallic Wars.**

Dio -   Cassius Dio: **History of Rome.**

Diodorus -   Diodorus Siculus: Diodorus of Sicily's historical library, translated by J.F. Wurm. Stuttgart 1827.

Herodian -   Herodian: **History of the Empire after Marcus Aurelius.**

Res Gestae -   Augustus: **Res Gestae.**

Suetonius -   Suetonius: **The Twelve Caesars.**

Agr -   Tacitus: **Agricola.**

Ann -   Tacitus: **Annals.**

Hist -   Tacitus: **Histories.**

Strabo -   Strabo: **A description of the world in seventeen volumes.**

Works Quoted In This Book & Suggested Further Reading

Allen, Origins
D.F. Allen: The Origins of Coinage in Britain: A Reappraisal. In: **Problems of the Iron Age in Southern Britain.** Ed. S.S. Frere. London 1961, 297-308.

Allen, Iceni
D.F. Allen: **The Coins of the Iceni.** Britannia 1, 1970, 1-33.

Allen, Cunobeline
D.F. Allen: **Cunobeline's Gold.** Britannia 6, 1975, 1-19.

Allen, Coins
D.F. Allen: **The Coins of the Ancient Celts.** Ed. D. Nash. Edinburgh 1980, 25-30.

Barrett
A. Barrett: Tiberius Claudius Cogidubnus and the Claudian Conquest. In: G. Webster, **Rome against Caratacus. The Roman Campaigns in Britain.** London 1981, 124-130.

Bechert
T. Bechert: **Die Provinzen des Römischen Reiches.** Einführung und Überblick. Mainz 1999, 161-166.

Birkhan
H. Birkhan: **Germanen und Kelten bis zum Ausgang der Römerzeit.** Der Aussagewert von Wörtern und Sachen für die frühesten keltisch-germanischen Kulturbeziehungen. Vienna 1970.

Birley, People
A. Birley: **The People of Roman Britain.** Berkeley, Los Angeles 1979.

Birley, Fasti
A. Birley: **The Fasti of Roman Britain.** Oxford 1981.

Birley, Britannien
A.R. Birley: Britannien. In: **Handbuch der europäien Wirtschafts- und Sozialgeschichte** Vol. 1. F. Vittinghoff et al. Stuttgart 1990, 537-555.

BMC
Catalogue of Greek Coins in the British Museum. 29 Vols. London 1873-1927.

Brodersen
K. Brodersen: **Das römische Britannien.** Darmstadt 1998.

CNG
Classical Numismatic Group, Inc.

De Jersey
P. de Jersey: **Celtic Coinage in Britain.** Princes Risborough 2001.

Demandt
A. Demandt: **Die Kelten.** Munich 1998.

Duval
P.M. Duval: **Die Kelten.** Munich 1978.

Ellis
P.B. Ellis: **Caesar's Invasion of Britain.** London 1978.

Fries-Knoblach
J. Fries-Knoblach: **Die Kelten.** Stuttgart 2002.

Herm
G. Herm: **Die Kelten. Das Volk, das aus dem Dunkel kam.** Reinbek 1977.

Hobbs
Richard Hobbs: **British Iron Age coins in the British Museum.** London 1996.

James
S. James: **Das Zeitalter der Kelten.** Düsseldorf 1996.

Jarrett
M.G. Jarrett: Setting the Scene. In: **A Companion to Roman Britain.** Ed. P.A. Clayton. Oxford 1980.

Jones
B. Jones, D. Mattingly: **An Atlas of Roman Britain.** Oxford 1990.

Kruta, Celts
V. Kruta: **The Celts of the West.** London 1985.

Kruta
V. Kruta: **Die Kelten. Aufstieg und Niedergang einer Kultur.** Freiburg 2000.

Künzl
E. Künzl: **Der römische Triumph. Siegesfeiern im antiken Rom.** Munich 1988.

Lengyel
L. Lengyel: **Das geheime Wissen der Kelten.** Freiburg 1990.

Leu
Leu Numismatics Ltd. Zürich.

Mack
R.P. Mack: **The Coinage of Ancient Britain.** London 1964.

Maier
B. Maier: **Die Religion der Kelten. Götter, Mythen, Weltbild.** Munich 2001.

Matschoss
M. Matschoss: Das religiöse Universum der Kelten. In: Geschichte 4, 2003, 40-43.

Moreau
J. Moreau: **Grosse Kulturen der Frühzeit. Die Welt der Kelten.** Stuttgart 1958.

Noelle
H. Noelle: **Die Kelten.** Pfaffenhofen 1974.

Overbeck
B. Overbeck: Die Münzen. Einführung in die Ausstellung. In: **Die Kelten in Mitteleuropa. Ausstellungskatalog Hallein.** Salzburg 1980, 101-110.

Parsons
C. Parsons: Boudicca. In: http://www.btinternet.com/~parsonal/boudicca.htm.

Peddie
J. Peddie: Invasion: **The Roman Conquest of Britain.** New York 1987.

Rudd
Chris Rudd, dealer specialising in Celtic coins, publishes illustrated monthly catalogue. Chris Rudd, PO Box 222, Aylsham, Norfolk NR11 6TY. Website: www.celticcoins.com

Salway
P. Salway: **Roman Britain.** Oxford, New York 1984.

Scarre
C. Scarre: **Die römischen Kaiser. Herrscher von Augustus bis Konstantin.** Augsburg 1998.

Seaby 1
H.A. Seaby: **Roman Silver Coins.** Vol. 1, the Republic to Augustus. London 1967.

Seaby 2
H.A. Seaby: **Roman Silver Coins.** Vol. 2, Tiberius to Commodus. London 1968.

Sear
D.R. Sear: **Greek Imperial Coins and their Values. The Local Coinage of the Roman Empire.** London 1997, 520-532.

Siemons
H. Siemons: St. Patricks Erben. In: Geschichte 4, 2003.

VA
R.D. van Arsdell: **Celtic Coinage of Britain.** London 1989.

Wacher
J. Wacher: **The Coming of Rome.** London 1979.

Webster
G. Webster: **Boudica: the British Revolt against Rome, AD 60.** London 1978.

Webster, Caratacus
G. Webster: **Roma against Caratacus. The Roman Campaigns in Britain.** London 1981.

Ziegaus, Jahrt.
B. Ziegaus: **Das keltische Münzwesen.** In: Das keltische Jahrtausend. Ed. H. Dannheimer. Exhibition catalogue. Munich 1993, 220-230.

Ziegaus, Geld
B. Ziegaus: **Das Geld der Kelten und ihrer Nachbarn. The collection of J. Schörghuber.** Exhibition catalogue Munich 1994/95. Munich 1994.

GREAT BOOKS FROM GREENLIGHT

BUTTONS & FASTENERS
500BC-AD1840
Gordon Bailey

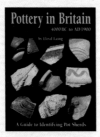
Pottery in Britain
4000BC to AD1900
by Lloyd Laing
A Guide to Identifying Pot Sherds

MEDIEVAL ENGLISH GROATS
Ivan Buck

Celtic & Roman Artefacts
Nigel Mills

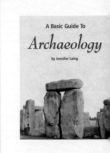
A Basic Guide To Archaeology
by Jennifer Laing

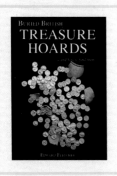
BURIED BRITISH TREASURE HOARDS
Edward Fletcher

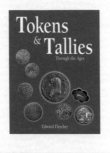
Tokens & Tallies
Through the Ages
Edward Fletcher

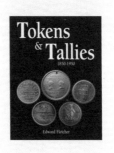
Tokens & Tallies
1850-1950
Edward Fletcher

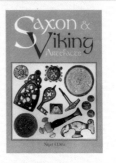
Saxon & Viking Artefacts
Nigel Mills

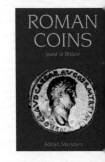
ROMAN COINS
found in Britain
Adrian Marsden

DETECTOR FINDS
Over 1,000 illustrations
Gordon Bailey

BUCKLES
1250-1800
Ross Whitehead

BEGINNER'S GUIDE METAL DETECTING
Julian Evan-Hart & Dave Stuckey

Medieval Artefacts
CATALOGUE AND PRICE GUIDE
Nigel Mills

Exploring Prehistoric & Roman England
by Barry M. Marsden
A guide to sites, monuments, artefacts and museums

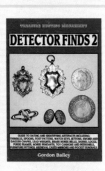
DETECTOR FINDS 2
Gordon Bailey

DETECTOR FINDS 3
Gordon Bailey

FINDS Identified
by Gordon Bailey
Price guide by Nigel Mills

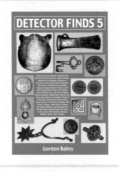
DETECTOR FINDS 5
Gordon Bailey

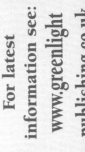
For latest information see:
www.greenlight publishing.co.uk

Benet's Artefacts
of England & the United Kingdom
STONE AGE
BRONZE AGE
IRON AGE
SAXON
MEDIEVAL
TUDOR

BRITISH BUTTONS
Civilian Uniform Buttons 19th-20th century
Dennis G Rice

Reading Beaches
Edward Fletcher's guide to identifying productive search areas

Reading Land
Edward Fletcher's guide to identifying productive search areas

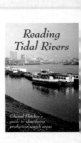
Reading Tidal Rivers
Edward Fletcher's guide to identifying productive search areas

Greenlight Publishing, 119 Newland Street, Witham, Essex CM8 1WF
Tel: 01376 521900 Fax: 01376 521901
email: books@greenlightpublishing.co.uk www.greenlightpublishing.co.uk

MasterCard
VISA